Mrs. Margaret A. Lindsell
79 El Cerrito Avenue
Hillsborough, CA 94010

To Peggy:
With very best wishes,
Judy J. Rankin
'76

A Natural Way to Golf Power

A Natural Way

to Golf Power

by JUDY RANKIN

WITH MICHAEL ARONSTEIN

Foreword by Bob Toski
Illustrations by Dom Lupo
Technical adviser—Dale Shankland

HARPER & ROW, PUBLISHERS
New York, Hagerstown,
San Francisco, London

FIRST EDITION

Designed by C. Linda Dingler

Library of Congress Cataloging in Publication Data

Rankin, Judy.
  A natural way to golf power.
  1. Golf.   2. Swing (Golf)   I. Aronstein, Michael.
II. Title.
GV965.R25   796.352'3   74-20407
ISBN 0-06-013517-4

To Bob Green and Eddie Held,
who helped me so much
before it seemed a reasonable thing to do

Contents

Foreword

I was first introduced to Judy Rankin through a business associate of mine in 1963. He had mentioned earlier, by phone, that this young lady had real potential as a future LPGA star, and asked that I spend some time analyzing her game.

I'll never forget meeting Judy when she arrived at the Miami airport. This tiny, freckle-faced girl walked toward me and I immediately said "oh God"—she is so small, she might get lost in an un-replaced divot. Little did I realize that an ounce of touch is worth a ton of brawn!

The first thing I noticed in Judy's game was her rather unorthodox left-hand position. I casually mentioned to her that if she intended to make a living in golf she might have to change her grip. She then told me in no uncertain terms that if I attempted to change her grip she'd be on the next plane out!

After watching her hit shots on the practice tee, I went out with her to play a round. On every hole Judy constantly drew the ball, even when some shots called for a fade. I remember one hole where the wind was blowing from right to left and the flagstick was placed in the right pocket of the green, which made it very difficult to hit a draw shot close. So I asked Judy to fade a few shots in. After a number of attempts to hit the ball left-to-right I said, "Judy, you can't hit the ball left-to-right with that grip, can you?" She readily admitted that she couldn't control that type of shot, but she still refused to change her grip.

Without changing her grip I proceeded to show her how to control the clubface through the ball, to put left-to-right spin on the shot. I was absolutely amazed to see the results she obtained without changing her grip—and how well she adapted to the change of swing plane that I advocated to make the ball fade. This reflected an inner confidence to me . . . a sign of future greatness. The rest, of course, is history.

Now Judy Rankin is without question, pound for pound, the finest player

I have ever seen. She combines great arm and hand speed with a superb lower body action to produce an unbelievable golf swing. Her lower body action through the ball is amazing. She utilizes it to the maximum, playing as well beneath herself as any player I have ever seen, with the exception of the great Mickey Wright. Every part of her body is playing an important role to produce the full effect of the clubhead against the ball. For a person her size to do this consistently and effectively, as she has, over a long period of time is tribute to her dedication to the art of mastering the golf swing.

Above all, she proved to me that you don't have to be fundamentally perfect to be successful. Judy is to golf what Bill Tilden, with his unorthodox grip, was to tennis. And just watching her must motivate many players, men and women alike, to the practice tee. She is an example of the maxim that if you're good enough, you're big enough to succeed.

More than all these things, Judy is a warm and affectionate woman. And she is appreciative and humble about her success. She had a long, tough road to success, and hasn't forgotten it. But she has no short memory—she has not forgotten the people who helped her get there. I have the deepest respect for her and hope her successes are as big and as great as her heart. She certainly deserves them.

Bob Toski, 1975

Acknowledgments

With many thanks to Gordon Marshall, who originally made the idea of a book reality; to Mike Aronstein and Dale Shankland for their writing and ability to understand my thoughts; and Dom Lupo for the beautiful artwork.

Also, to my husband and son for making the time I needed possible, and last to my father, who helped me for many years to understand what I do and why it works.

I
Golfing
Backgrounds

1

My Game of Golf

With the extraordinary growth of golf in recent years, a great deal of instructional material has appeared in an attempt to satisfy the unique demands of individual classes of golfers. I assure you that I would not be adding to this huge body of instructional literature if I didn't honestly feel as though I had some sort of fresh perspective to offer. Certain of my ideas may run contrary to existing thoughts about golf technique. That doesn't bother me one bit. My competitive record speaks well of my personal method; and besides, it seems as though too many teaching theories are based on the assumption that the average weekend player can, if he or she works hard enough, build a swing that is similar to Jack Nicklaus's or Arnold Palmer's. This does not sound reasonable to me. The vast majority of amateurs, both male and female, are more closely related to me in terms of physical aptitude than they are to the male touring pros. I think that they would do well to give my fundamentals a good look. If any of you are worried about learning a woman's method, consider this: Pound for pound, I may very well be one of the longest hitters in golf. There you have it. The key to my method is **power.** At 5'3" and 108 lbs., I have been forced to develop a style of swinging the club that produces maximum yardage per pound. It is this style that I intend to share with you.

As far as I can tell, the modern trend in golf instruction is to emphasize restriction, to eliminate a large part of the motion that was considered essential for a good swing not too many years ago. I was taught basic fundamentals, like a big turn, a good transfer of weight and a free swinging action. A lot of these aren't taught anymore. Now, most of the things that are being taught cannot be understood by my neighbors down the block.

I think that an awful lot of today's teaching methods are faddish, and will come and go very quickly, as "Square to Square" did. That method destroyed quite a number of good players. When your instructional ideas become that difficult, you tend to produce a golf swing that is very difficult, very complex. Since the game itself requires so much thought, it seems to me that if the player is not burdened with all sorts of involved thoughts about his or her swing, more attention can be paid to the matter at hand: producing a good score. When you're out on a golf course, your mind is working on what club to choose, which route to take into a green or what's the best way to try for a birdie on this par 5. With all of these elements to consider, there's no time to stop and think about the various aspects of your golf swing, especially if that swing is unnatural. A fairly natural movement is more easily repeated by the muscles, and thus does not require so much thought. Many of the moves that I will describe further on in the book are things that a poor player or a beginner can understand and learn to do.

My game of golf developed more or less through trial and error. Throughout my life, my father has been my number-one teacher. He is a weekend player, and his strongest point as a golfer is his love for the game. After a lot of plotting on my part, he let me try hitting balls and from then on we learned the game together. Actually, as a teacher he learned the game better than I, but now, some twenty years later, I believe I understand what we were striving for then. I was only six years old, and when you think of it, a beginning golfer has no more knowledge of the golf swing than a six-year-old. So, if everything is put in very simple, basic terms—exactly the way it was put to me—the beginner has a better chance of understanding. Now understanding something and being able to do it are two different things, but I have learned that those players with a sound knowledge of the game have a substantial advantage when it comes to maintaining a golf swing. One thing that I've noticed in good players is an ability to abide by the simple mechanical thoughts that they have used throughout their careers. When a good golfer gets to playing poorly, he or she is not striving to learn something new about the golf swing. No one, myself included, will try to find a new system or a little gimmick to straighten out his game. You simply try to return to the good, simple fundamentals that are easy and that work so well. A number of younger players on tour, along with most weekend amateurs, have not learned the beauty of a basic approach to the game of golf. Every day they turn to a new system, always thinking that they're not hitting the ball because some magical move is missing. When you begin doing this, nothing about your swing becomes familiar and all of a sudden you're absolutely lost.

I always keep notes of my key thoughts. My father has kept some notes for me at various times when I have come to him in the midst of a slump. And we've always managed to find the mistakes that were creeping into my action and causing me to play poorly. I keep track of those little mistakes. I also try to make notes at times when I am hitting the ball very well. You would be surprised at some of the very basic things that I go back to twenty-four years later for help. The Triple Crown, in January 1975, was a good example. I really had to work hard during a short span of time to prepare myself for that tournament. The weather in Midland, Texas, was not that good and I worked as much as I could in the cold weather, but when I got to Florida I was by no means ready. I finally reached a point where I was hitting the ball well, but even so I found that every sixth or seventh shot I would lose everything and hit the ball miles off to the right. Now there's no way that you can hope to play tournament golf if you hit one out of every six shots off into never-never land. I was getting pretty frantic about the whole thing, and I dreaded the thought of things going like that once the tournament began. It appeared as though this periodic wildness was simply the result of some bad timing, since I was striking the majority of my shots fairly well. So I went back to one of the most basic things that I ever learned about golf—moving everything away from the ball in one piece. I find that this thought creates a good starting base from which to establish some sort of workable timing pattern. I went back to this simple key and managed to play through the entire tournament without hitting any bad shots to the right. If you build a fairly simple golf swing, it is possible to make a fairly simple correction when things go bad.

When I began learning the game, my father would take me out to a driving range and make certain that the fundamental elements were correct. Though I have a very strong grip right now, I started out with an orthodox grip and a fundamentally sound address posture. I would take a wood and stand on the tee and make about a third of a swing, a few feet back and then through. I just sort of bopped the ball out off the end of the tee, and I did that until I had the basic motion mastered, until my father thought that it was correct. As I progressed I would take it back a bit farther each time, and pretty soon we had built a golf swing. I didn't begin simply by swinging at the ball and then making all sorts of adjustments and corrections. We built the swing from the bottom up, from its simplest form into a full, usable action. So the basic swing that I learned never had very many mistakes in it; we never let it get so far off track that a real flaw would develop. Things were done right the first time. After assembling a basic swing, all that was left for me to develop was a method of playing the various shots needed to score well.

I suppose there are different routes that one can travel when putting together a golf game. I can assume that I have some sort of natural ability —I have a certain talent for golf, but I am not an all-round athlete. I am athletic where golf is concerned, but I don't do other things very well. My golfing talent allows me to change things and make adjustments more readily than the average player. Someone may tell me to do something and immediately I will be able to do it without having them explain in detail or demonstrate. So there must be a type of natural feel for the swing at work within my physical makeup. Yet I have seen good players who have almost no natural feel for the game. They have succeeded in manufacturing a mechanical swing through sheer determination and hard work. There are other people who never manage to build a top golf game, even though they appear to have a good deal of inborn ability. In all facets of life there are people who have to work harder than others to achieve a certain goal. It is one of those things that just happens to be.

The person with natural talent has a bit of an advantage in starting out if he or she is able to combine ability with hard work. I don't think that you can bank on getting by solely on ability, although there are those who at times can succeed purely on the basis of some tremendous natural feel. But those players who get to the top and stay there are testimony to the value of determined effort. Kathy Whitworth is an example of a player who has relied to a large extent upon feel and natural sensitivity. But even Kathy, who does have this extraordinary gift for the game, has reached the top and stayed there through determination and lots of hard work. Even though she's never done things quite the way people thought she should, she has been able to carry it off very well. Her natural feel has rescued her, time and time again. All the determination in the world could not have kept Kathy on top for so long had she not been blessed with this great gift for feeling just what a golf club was doing as she moved it through her golf swing. Yet she still has to work on maintaining a golf swing to provide her with a medium through which she can express all of this ability. What you're aiming for in terms of a championship golfer is, ideally, someone who is gifted with a great amount of feel for the game and is willing to work very hard to take every advantage of his or her natural ability. And with all of the very talented people on both tours, I still don't know that there is anyone who is playing up to full potential. The people who are determined enough to put in all of the hard work are the ones that come the closest. They become and remain champions. There's no doubt that the finest players have a great deal of talent—but the thing about them that is most impressive is not so much their talent but their determination.

2

Life as a
Tournament Player

I began playing in local junior tournaments around St. Louis when I was about seven, and continued my involvement in junior golf well on into my teens. Junior golf is a very important thing insofar as it helps to maintain an interest in the game beyond practice and casual play. Even if a young golfer expects to work for ten or fifteen years to train for a life in golf, it's difficult to keep up a reasonable level of enthusiasm unless there are events to look forward to and work toward. I always had two or three events every year that I tried to establish as goals for that particular year, and these helped a great deal in keeping my competitive spirits high. One of the most important things to be had from an association with junior golf competition is the development of a proper attitude. Golf's a character builder, and junior golf teaches a child to take the good with the bad, the bad with the good. It was a great help to me in my attempts to build a competitive game, since I was constantly reminded of the need for a proper outlook and a positive mental approach.

I joined the LPGA tour when I was seventeen. When I first came out I was very much in awe of the entire business. It was scary. In almost no time at all I had lost most of the confidence in my game that I'd developed in the course of my junior career. I think that I was a good player as an amateur, and it doesn't seem, in retrospect, as though my game changed so drastically after I became a professional. It was almost uncanny, but somehow I simply lost my ability to perform as a golfer. I don't mean to say that I was horribly bad, but I never managed to do anything that was particularly impressive.

One of the things that may have hurt me as a young professional was that as a junior and teen-age player, I didn't lose very often—and when I did, it was mainly on account of some flash of stupidity on my part. Compared to that, the tour was a whole new ball game. I was encouraged by a lot of different people who told me that I had the ability to earn money out there and win. Yet I don't think that I ever really believed it. I had to get used to the fact that on given days there were a number of players who were simply going to beat me. I was very discouraged at first, and I got down on myself and my own future as a golfer. I can't say that there was no fun in it all— there were some good times—but I played in only about nine tournaments that first year, and I was a little homesick, to tell the truth. Looking back, I see that I didn't quite have the powers of concentration then to perform much better than I actually did. I hit the ball very well in some of those early tournaments. I simply could not settle down enough to do anything with it as far as scoring was concerned. My age actually had a lot to do with it. I see girls come out on the tour now; some of them are very young and yet I haven't seen too many who are lacking in confidence. The entire atmosphere is different these days. The year that I came out there was a group of young players—Carol Mann, Sandra Haynie and myself—all just a year or two apart. We were in awe of the older, more established stars and suffered a lot when our games didn't measure up to theirs. It seems that the young players coming up today have adopted a different lifestyle. That's not to say that some of them don't work very hard on their games. They merely take things in stride much better. None of them appear to be in a frantic rush to get anywhere, and it takes some sort of catastrophe to get them down. They never seem to be discouraged. I think part of the confidence that new players have today stems from the fact that boys and girls seem to be maturing at an earlier age. Lately there has been a trend toward building up the newly emerging players much more than was the case when I was breaking in. A young player today can count on a rash of complimentary publicity if she has any reputation prior to joining the tour. And there are no new young players who have become greats as of yet. But the build-ups that they receive are good as far as their confidence is concerned. I don't believe that the new girls today have a greater knowledge or understanding of the game than we had back then. They just appear to have more success, in a shorter span of time, than we did. There are also many more girls coming out to play.

There is a good deal more incentive for the younger player these days to prepare for a career on the tour. There is much more to be gained by doing well on the women's tour now than there was back in the early sixties. With the rise in popularity experienced by the LPGA in recent years, life for a young player is somewhat more interesting. Expansion of media coverage has increased the excitement surrounding each individual tournament, and, as more people become familiar with women's golf, the flavor of life out on the tour becomes more appealing.

When I started out on the tour, there were perhaps thirty players, in all, competing. Now there are more than a hundred at many tournament sites. The competition has become keener as more girls are attracted by the rewards offered for success. The marginal player cannot survive very well these days. The tour is a bit more of a job now, and golf is a bit more like work. If you let yourself down and don't perform well, you lose much more in terms of potential reward. Although we may have been overly dramatic in my early days, it always seemed to us as though we had suffered a tremendous loss whenever something went wrong. In a sense, we took things too seriously, and often we would attack our problems from the wrong standpoint. But the girls today are a different breed, and I'm certain that it's true of the young players on the men's tour. They are studious and very serious about their games, and yet they have an ability to leave golf on the golf course and build a more diverse spectrum of interests and activities. It was much more of a twenty-four-hour-a-day thing with us in my early days. Our entire lives were centered around golf, and our spirits rose and fell with our fortunes on the course. There was little else to turn to. Now it's possible to play golf on the course and do other things away from the course, which perhaps is a very healthy thing and explains most of the positive changes in the attitudes of young players.

There were very few new players coming out at the time I joined the tour, so in essence I was alone when I began. I was fortunate in that there were enough young people out on tour for me to make some friends. Today there are many more players, both established players and emerging players, and it is not such a lonely place to be. Again, the young girls today have more people and more outside interests to turn to as a relief from the strain of competitive golf.

Even today, after fourteen years as a professional player, I find it difficult to leave my feelings on the golf course when the round is done. Sometimes I'll talk over a bad round with Yippy, my husband, and other times I'll go off by myself and sulk. Sulking is not a good thing for anyone, but I usually find that I don't make the same mistake twice. I tend to get very angry with myself and I want to be left alone, but often some good will emerge from it.

The most annoying rounds are the ones in which I've hit the ball well, putted reasonably well, stayed away from any serious blunders and have still managed to shoot myself out of contention. Usually it's a matter of a few mental errors costing me a good round. Not too long ago I had such a round that was especially rankling: the day was perfect, the course was not that difficult, and I shot 74. Under those conditions, 74 was more like 78 relative to the remainder of the field. It sounds like a respectable score, but I could not have been more disgusted. And I didn't even fall down in one particular area of the game—I played many holes very well, even hit the pin twice during the round, and my putting was fair. But plain mental blunder had me off track early in the round and I never managed to recover from it. I got angry at myself and angry at the situation that I was in. I drove into a fairway bunker on a straightforward par 4, and although I wasn't too pleased with having driven the ball in the sand, I counted on having a relatively simple shot of about 120 yards out of the bunker to the green. Instead, the ball was up under the lip of the trap and I was faced with a difficult shot just trying to move the ball out of the sand. As I stood there and looked at that predicament, I simply wanted to explode, since the same thing had happened to me the week before. In the previous tournament I had played a very good shot down the first fairway, and I was in a position from which I could just about reach the green on this par 5 in two. There was a large trap right in front of the green, but that was of little consequence since I felt that I might be able to make a birdie even from the sand. So I just blasted one right at the green, thinking that even if I wound up in the trap it would be no big matter. Well, the ball went into the bunker, and when I reached it it was sitting in this little area where there happened to be a natural wall built up. The ball was right up against this wall. There I was, after hitting two good shots, after thinking out my game plan thoroughly, yet in a spot from which I couldn't even play out backwards. I almost broke my wrist trying to blast out. So when the exact same thing happened during the first round of the next week's tournament, I was what you might call quite irritated. I had these awful flashes of every shot that rolled into a trap finding its way into an unplayable lie. So I stood there, fuming and feeling sorry for myself—bad policy, since things of that sort are as they are and can't be changed after the fact. In any event, I did manage to scrape the ball out of that lie and make a bogey on the hole, which should not have been that disastrous. But I carried that resentment over my bad luck with me for another hole, and I made a second bogey and let the whole round go right down the drain . . . all because of my inability to think sensibly and regard everything from a proper perspective. The whole thing was merely the result of a mental error. And although you and I both will have some days like that, there was just no excuse for my attitude. None at all. Disastrous things happen many times on one hole, but I find that when I'm thinking well I can leave all my bad thoughts on that hole, and go on to the next with a clear head.

In any case, I do get very upset with myself when I'm not playing well, and if my problems appear to stem from a mistake in my swing pattern, then I become very concerned. Any good player is able to tell when he or she has struck the ball well simply by the feeling at impact. You know the feeling that you are striving for when trying to play a certain shot, and that feeling either emerges at impact or it does not. If you have to make adjustments in your swing to get the clubface on the ball, all is not well mechanically. When I play poorly for this reason, I worry a great deal about my swing, but I am not as upset as when I waste a day of potentially fine golf because of mental mistakes. I feel as though I'm a good player, but I don't like to spot the leaders six shots in the first round of a tournament. It's just not that easy.

I really have the same group of friends out on the tour that I've always had. I don't spend quite so much time with my friends now that I'm married and have a family. Marlene Hagge, Pam Higgins, and Carol Mann are all friends. There's a small group of us out there, and we've always spent a good bit of time together. Now I spend somewhat more time with Kathy Cornelius, because our children are nearly the same age and they've been together often.

There are very few people playing with me on the tour whom I allow to advise me regarding my golf swing. I don't even want to hear what anyone has to say on the matter. Unsolicited advice sometimes raises questions in your mind about your own swing, and doubts are the last thing that *anyone* needs out here. I might, from time to time, ask a friend to check and see where I'm aiming. But I wouldn't allow anyone to work on the character of my own particular swing. That's simply the way I feel about it, and I've had more or less the same sentiments ever since I came on tour. If I do feel as though I'm getting into serious trouble where my swing is concerned, the best thing for me is to leave the tour and try to find the problem. And that's when I go to my father. We always revert to the fundamental ideas that have been so important to my game throughout the years. We can generally pick out one aspect of my action that seems not to be working properly at the time, such as a smooth takeaway or a good turn. Many times when I've felt as though I was hitting the ball tolerably well my father has caught the beginning symptoms of a basic flaw, and worked with me to correct it. As I gain experience, I am getting better at helping myself with some of the problems. Still, you're never able to see yourself while you are making a correction. You can only proceed by feel and results. It's very reassuring to have someone around to act as a mirror, someone who knows your swing inside-out, someone you trust. At times, when I'm on the course and seemingly hitting the ball well, I find that all of a sudden I'm not getting as much distance as I should. Out on the course, where I have to do my own repair work, one little change like checking to see that I'm extending the club to make a big arc to the top can bring back that lost power during the course of a round. Most of the learning that I do now is a matter of returning to the good simple things that have always been with me. I don't waste much time hunting for something new.

3

A Winning Edge

To win on the professional tour, you must feel as though you are capable of winning. Remember that only you can control what you do. You must have a certain amount of confidence in your abilities as a golfer. In a sense, you have to be somewhat self-centered to become a winner—at least insofar as your golf game is concerned. The top players never seem to worry about their fellow competitors' games; they have enough faith in their own abilities to forget about what's going on about them and settle down to the task of winning.

Winners appear to play their best golf while under pressure, and that's a function of a person's ability to dispense with all sorts of conscious thought and allow the automatic pilot—"muscle memory"—to assume control. This is not to say that the victor is not nervous or that the player who is in strong contention during the final few holes does not feel the pressure. They are merely able to control themselves, and they can function skillfully under the circumstances. People often forget that pressure is strictly an internal commodity, a person's own interior response to the situation at hand. At times you hear people speak of pressure as though it were a tangible entity, when in fact it has no more substance than anger or fear or joy. Pressure is a product of your own mind and, as such, can be controlled and dealt with readily if you are willing to devote your mind to the effort. It takes some mental training. I do believe that some personalities by nature are more emotional than others—maybe myself included. This makes the job of controlling your mind a little tougher.

The best players in golf always give the impression that they are in complete control at all times, that they are the masters of their own destinies. Even when they don't win they leave you with the feeling that they have done all that was possible under the circumstances, that they didn't allow a bad attitude to ruin a round. If a talented golfer is able to give his or her best effort every time out, that golfer will eventually come out on top. It will be just a matter of time before things fall into place.

As much as some people will deny the importance of luck as an influence in championship golf, I think that luck does play a certain role in determining the winner of any particular tournament. Actually, it's not so much a question of good luck but rather the avoidance of any bad luck, if you catch the distinction. At times your ability can carry you through without any unusually lucky things helping you along, but very bad luck is something that I find ruinous. When all conditions are the same for all players, half an inch can determine who wins and who does not. You can plug up in the bank of a trap or you can barely clear it and roll all the way to the hole. You can be the greatest player in the game and yet I'm certain that you can't control the flight of a golf ball to a degree of inches. I'm not after any extraordinary good luck, but I'm always hoping that I can avoid the very bad things, things that you don't ordinarily take into account when considering the risk involved in playing a given shot, such as a bird flying into your ball and causing it to drop in a pond (to use an extreme example). During one tournament in Los Angeles I had a 6- or 7-iron into a green and the pin was tucked way over on the right corner. At this particular tournament the gallery ropes came right up to the edge of the green rather than flaring out as they normally do. I hit a very good shot and the ball was floating right down at the flag, looking like a near-perfect stroke . . . but instead of dropping near the hole, the ball hit one of the gallery ropes dead in the center and rebounded way off the green. I had nearly a full wedge left to get back. That's what I mean by bad luck. When you hit the ball into a bunker and it sticks up under a lip, you've had a touch of bad luck. The intended penalty for hitting into a sand trap is generally based on the simple fact that you'll have to play your next shot from sand. Sand traps were not designed with the intention of giving you an unplayable lie. So when I do get an unplayable lie in the sand, I consider myself somewhat less than fortunate. It may well be true that the good luck balances the bad in the long run, but it seems that the winner of any single tournament has generally not had much bad luck. Things have more or less gone according to schedule. In any event, when you adopt an attitude about luck, remember that the root cause of anything that happens to your golf ball is *you*. You hit it to begin with. That's the only thing that you can do, physically, to influence the outcome of a shot, so it's the only thing that you should worry about. Stay calm and resolute, and let the chips fall as they may.

The Colgate-European Open at Sunningdale, England was without a doubt one of my biggest wins ever. My key thought throughout that tournament was to place the ball in the fairway, because Sunningdale is a brutal course if you are not keeping the ball in play. It was one of those weeks when I found myself swinging very well, so all I had to concentrate on was making solid contact, hitting the ball clearly and off the center of the clubface. I was thinking about that down to the very last shot at Sunningdale, and it worked beautifully for me. I was really hitting the ball with a great deal of control and confidence. There was one particular shot on the last day that I remember as being a good illustration of this point. The sixteenth hole was a very long par 4, and with the wind in our faces, as it was during the final round, there was no way that it could be reached in two shots. There were fairway bunkers sitting about fifty yards in front of the green up on a little hill, so that if you find them you are left with a very difficult shot into the green. I was playing with Betsy Cullen, and Betsy hit what appeared to be a very good second shot, but she still couldn't get over the sand. I had driven a bit longer, and I had a downhill lie. I knew that I was leading at this point, but I didn't know my margin. So I had a pretty important decision to make with that second shot. At the time, this seemed to be a key hole for me. I knew that I could not hit a high shot, because the wind would blow it right back in my face, and a low shot would never carry the bunkers going up the hill. I suppose that, in fact, I was faced with the prospect of either hitting a nearly perfect 3-wood or playing my third shot from the sand. I decided to play the 3-wood, and the sole thought in my mind at the time was to make precise contact. I hit about as good a shot as I ever have, and the ball cleared the bunkers nicely and left me with a very easy little chip to the hole. That may have clinched the tournament right there. With all of the long fairway shots to play over there, the simple thought of meeting the ball solidly and staying with the shot—being conscious of the clubhead following the ball out toward the target—helped me immeasurably. In this most complex of games, it's the simple things that count toward winning.

II
Foundations
of a
Power Game

4

A Natural Power Grip

Anyone who is at all familiar with the golf swing would, upon seeing me play, notice that my left hand grip is noticeably "stronger" than the grip that is commonly thought of as correct for the modern golfer. I guess that in many ways the strong grip is responsible for the simplicity of my entire golf swing. Throughout this chapter, when I refer to the strength of a golf grip, I will be referring to the degree to which the hands are placed over or under the grip of a club. A strong grip is one in which the hands are turned to the right on the club, with the left hand over the top of the club and the right hand underneath. A weak grip finds the hands turned to the left, so that the back of the left hand is pointing to the intended target and the right hand is more over than under the club.

The strength of the grip is important because it dictates the amount of rotation in the hands through impact, which in turn controls the position of the clubface and establishes the entire pattern of the swing. When speaking of the grip in general terms, the relative strength or weakness of the hand position is, in itself, not the only important question. Of great importance is finding a grip that allows you to return your hands, and thus the clubface, to their starting position time and time again. And it seems to me that the more natural the starting position of the hands, the easier it will be for the player to return to that position during the golf swing.

If you stand naturally with your arms hanging at your sides without any conscious effort to manipulate the position of your hands, you'll find that the back of your left hand is facing almost in front of you, rather than directly to your left, and at least three of the knuckles across the back of the hand will be visible. That's why a strong left-hand position in a golf grip feels so natural for most people. It happens to be the way the hands and arms naturally orient themselves when they are allowed to hang freely.

The position of my left hand is, as previously mentioned, a strong one in traditional terms. My right hand, however, is in a traditionally orthodox or neutral position, the palm of the hand facing more or less directly toward the target, the right hand reaching forward to the club. My reasoning in putting together a grip of this sort is fairly simple. The left hand has a different role in the golf swing than the right, and thus the two hands should be placed on the grip to allow each to perform its proper task. The left hand, and the left side of the body for that matter, act as the "pullers" during the golf swing. They are applying all of their energy from a position "in front" (more toward the target) than the right side. Because the left hand leads the right side to the ball, it establishes the entire path of the downswing, and must be placed in a position of definite control. The left side, during a golf swing, acts somewhat like the lead horse in a team. The leader sets the pace and the direction; everything else follows in that pattern. If the leader loses stride, the whole team is thrown off. With this thought in mind, I place my left hand in as strong a position as possible.

What surprises me about modern-day golf instruction is that a strong left-hand position should be considered unorthodox. Every golf magazine and instruction book that I pick up these days is reiterating the theory that golf is a left-sided game. If we accept this premise, then it becomes more difficult than ever for me to believe the modern emphasis on a weak left-hand grip. The biggest problem for a right-handed player is that the right side is too strong in relation to the left to allow the left to be used as the leader. So I can't understand why there is such a trend toward weakening the left-hand position, because by weakening your left-hand position you give your right hand every opportunity in the world to overtake it during the swing. If you truly believe, as I do, that the left side is the guiding light in the golf swing, then you ought to do as I do and give your left hand every possible advantage by placing it in as strong a position on the club as is practical. Your hands are about the most important part of your body when it comes to controlling the golf club. They are your only direct link with the club. So they should be set in a position that allows them to work most efficiently and most naturally.

The player who discounts the validity of the strong left-hand grip simply on the basis of what he has seen and heard from the touring pros and teachers is just not being realistic. The golfers on tour are strong, well-practiced professional athletes who spend the greater part of their lives conditioning the specific muscles that are used for the golf swing.

If you were to pick up a hammer and attempt to drive a nail into a board,

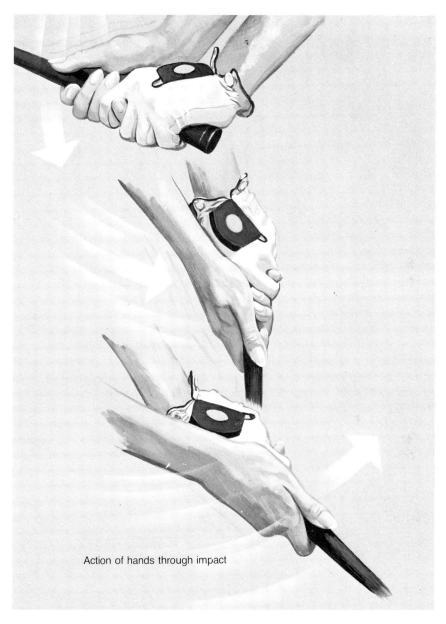

Action of hands through impact

The action of the hands through impact. Because the heel of the left hand is set in a leading position at the outset and kept in that position throughout the swing, there is no need to rotate or manipulate the hands in the impact area. The release of the hands is simply an uncocking of the wrists, with the palm of the right hand driving directly toward the target as the wrists release.

you would hold the hammer so that the heel of your left hand was facing toward the nail—as though you were preparing to strike the nail with a karate chop. You would never grip the hammer so that the back of your hand was facing your target. With the heel of your hand leading, you can hit the head of the nail more easily and also drive it farther into the board. If you tried to do it with the back of your hand facing the nail, you'd probably miss altogether. I think that the same theory holds true for the golf swing. It seems much easier for the hands to transmit power to the ball if they are set in a position that will allow them to return to the ball with the heel of the left hand facing the target. As I see it, the orthodox impact position with the back of the left hand facing the target places that hand in a very unsteady position, because most golfers do not have sufficient strength across the back of the left wrist to control the club. With the heel of the left hand leading, there is no way for the hand and wrist to break down at impact and allow the right side to "flip" through the ball. Many tour players have a stronger left-hand grip than you are led to believe.

In any golf swing, good or bad, there is a certain point at which the wrists break into a cocked position. A good cocked position is one in which the back of the left wrist and forearm are in the same plane, with the wrist hinged at the base of the thumb. The great advantage of my grip is the elimination of the need to rotate the hands during the swing. With my strong left-hand grip, I begin with the hands in a position where they can cock naturally with no rotation during the backswing. With a weak left-hand grip, the hands and arms must rotate during the backswing to arrive at a proper cocking position at the top. Then, during the downswing, there must be some rotation in the opposite direction to allow the clubface to square. Most amateurs find it very difficult to accomplish the needed release with a weak grip, and most of them slice as a result. My method eliminates that particular problem.

I begin with the back of my left hand parallel to the proper swing plane, and I hold it in that position throughout my swing. With a conventional, weak left-hand grip, the back of the left hand begins perpendicular to rather than parallel to the swing plane. This necessitates some sort of rotation, some manipulation of the hands to place them in a natural cocking position, and that just complicates the golf swing.

One of the most mystifying aspects of the swing for the average player is the rotation of the hands and arms through impact to bring the clubface to a square position at the ball. So many average players slice because they simply don't have the control required in the left side to promote this rotational motion through the ball. They are constantly arriving at impact with the clubface open and the hands only partially released. With my method, the hands and arms are *never* rotated away from the ball, so there is no need for any rotation to square the clubface during the downswing. You begin with the heel of your left hand pointing in the direction that you want the clubhead to travel, and all through the golf swing this relationship is maintained. The heel of your left hand represents the clubface, and it is always pointing down the desired swing path. It is that simple.

So far, in terms of the grip, I have only spoken of the left hand and the desired dominance of the left side during the swing. This should not be taken to mean that your right side has nothing to do with hitting a golf ball. Although many teachers still contend that the left side provides everything in the golf swing, I have to disagree, because I think that proper use of the right side adds a great deal of strength to the swing. The right hand is also important as a guiding influence, particularly for the weekend player who has not had the time to strengthen the left side sufficiently. The right hand is, for the right-handed golfer, the "seeker" hand. The left hand and left side of the body are responsible for leading the entire swing, but the right hand has a greater degree of feel for determining the exact location of the clubhead. The left hand may bring the right to the ball, but it is the right hand that actually has the feeling for placing the clubhead on the ball. And, because the proper address position finds the right hand reaching somewhat for the club, the right hand should be placed on the club in a weaker position than the left, with the palm of the hand facing the target. This allows the right hand to act most effectively as the "seeker" throughout the swing. Again, the right hand has a different function in the swing than the left. If used properly, it can add a great deal of power to the swing during the later stages. Also, for most right-handed players, the right hand is more sensitive and can be used very effectively in producing solid contact. With this in mind, it is placed in a different position on the grip.

Regardless of what a lot of people say or think, this grip will not necessarily result in your hitting a whole bunch of badly hooked shots. The only way that you'll hook the ball with this grip is if you are exaggeratedly right-handed or simply unable to maintain the motion of your hands through impact. The player who hits and quits, who stops the lead of the left hand at impact, will probably hit a number of bad hooks, because quitting at impact allows the right hand to overtake the left and flip over it, shutting the face of the club. In the same vein, a person who quits at impact with a weaker grip will probably hit the ball way to the right. What my grip does is to make the player pay particular attention to two of the most important swing fundamentals: swinging through rather than at the ball, and letting the clubhead extend out toward the target after the ball is on its way. In any case, there are very few weekend players, men or women, who have a great problem with a hook. If I were a weekend player, no matter what my handicap, I would want to be able to hook the ball rather than hit a slice or a fade all day. Most women hit the ball from left to right simply because they know of no other way to hit it. And because the woman golfer's biggest problem is a lack of length off the tee, every woman should learn how to hit a hook or at least a draw. She will immediately have ten more yards off the tee. It's not until you reach the level of a scratch player that you need concern yourself with hitting a fade. Most good players have the ability to hook the ball, whether they choose to play a draw or a fade out on the course. So, before you concern yourself with the problem of hitting a fade, learn how to hit a draw.

In my experience with club players, I find that almost invariably they hit a great many short, weak slices because no one has ever been able to teach them a proper action with the hands. You can go out to the tees at any country club and watch player after player hit a perfect little banana-ball because they have no idea how to get their hands to a square position at the ball. With my grip, these people should be able to forget about their hands and develop a more powerful right-to-left game. I remember one lady whom I showed my grip to who came running into the clubhouse screaming about drives that had gone ten to fifty yards further *the very first time* that she turned her left hand over on the club. Now I don't know how this woman was hitting the ball to begin with—she may have been driving it ten yards—but her excitement was a pretty phenomenal thing, considering that she had tried the grip for only one round.

In light of my experiences with women players, I believe that I can take a man who is a fairly good golfer, teach him this grip in a few moments, and have him hitting the ball stronger than he ever did. If you watch on the LPGA tour, you will notice that there are an awful lot of players with very strong left-hand grips. There are many players who grip the club in almost exactly the same fashion as I do, but because I've always played with this sort of grip I'm the one who is singled out as the golfer with the strong grip. Be that as it may, I still can't understand why, if a small person like me can hit the ball an unusually long way with my grip, a larger person can't hit the ball enormous distances using this same method. There seems to be no logical reason. I would love to see a tall, strong person give my method a try, because I think that the proportional gain in distance would hold true for him.

As you look at the illustrations of my grip in this book, you will notice that my wrist seems to be in a somewhat abnormal position. This is because I grip the club even more strongly than I would recommend for the average player. My grip has become somewhat exaggerated over the years, but my

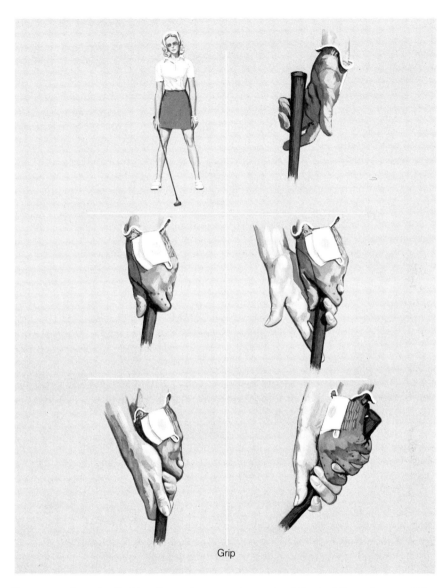

Grip

To assume the grip, first lay the club across the roots of the last three fingers of the left hand, then fold the entire hand OVER the club so that three and a half or four of the knuckles across the back of the left hand are visible. The right hand holds the club in the roots of the middle fingers, with the thumb and forefinger around the grip in modified "pistol" fashion. The palm of the right hand faces directly toward your target, and the thumb of the left hand should be snugly covered by the pad of the right thumb. If your left thumb is visible after you have gripped the club, your right hand is too far underneath the shaft.

left arm is conditioned to a degree where it can take the strain. As a teacher, I am trying to propose a method that will apply to the greatest number of golfers; I'm not trying to teach everyone to play golf exactly as I do.

To assume the proper left-hand grip on the club, hold your left hand in front of you with the palm facing upward, the fingers extended, and your fingertips pointed slightly to your left. Now take the grip of the club and lay it across the palm of your hand just below the roots of the last three fingers. The club should cross your index finger just beyond the base joint. With the club held in this position, simply fold the palm of your hand over the top of the grip so that the back of the hand is almost completely visible. You should be able to see three and a half or possibly all four knuckles across the back of the hand. The club is held firmly against the palm of the hand by the last three fingers.

To assume the proper right-hand position on the club, hold your right hand in front of you, with the palm facing upward, the fingers extended, and the fingertips pointing directly to your left. Simply lay the grip of the club across the roots of your middle and ring fingers and close your hand around the grip so that the palm faces directly toward your left. The "V" formed by your right thumb and forefinger should point to the right of your nose. Pressure in the right hand is maintained by the middle and ring fingers. The thumb and forefinger should be pressed together at the point where they join, in a pistol grip, and the tips of these fingers should rest very lightly on the club to prevent any early pickup with the right hand at the beginning of the backswing.

You are probably wondering at this point what is to be done with the little finger on the right hand. Interlock, overlap, or what? Well, to tell the truth, I use a variation of the standard positions that may best be termed an "overlock" grip. I find that my hands mesh together very comfortably if I place the little finger of my right hand between the forefinger and middle finger of the left so that the tip of the little finger is actually resting on the grip of the club. This grip allows me to get all of my fingers on the club while keeping the hands properly united. I do have long slender fingers which makes this quite easy. If you find this is uncomfortable for you, don't worry, because it is a minor part of the overall grip.

When looking at your completed grip, you should be able to see all four knuckles across the back of your left hand, and only the knuckle above the forefinger should be visible on the right hand. The little finger on the right hand sits between the middle finger and forefinger of the left hand. The left thumb is firmly encased by the natural pocket formed beneath the base of the right thumb. If you are able to see your left thumb when standing at address, then your right hand is in too strong a position, too far under the club.

The hands should feel united on the club. Pressure in the left hand is maintained by the last three fingers and especially the little finger. Pressure in the right hand is in the first three fingers, and the upper part of the right thumb is pressed firmly against the fleshy part of the hand above the base of the forefinger, forming the pistol grip with those two fingers.

5

Alignment: Setting Up the Swing

I try very hard to set up the same way each time. The first thing that I always do is to get behind the ball, to visualize the flight pattern of my shot to the target, whether that target is the flag or a spot in the fairway. I think that you can get a clearer picture of the line from behind the ball as opposed to alongside of it. So my first step in setting up is actually a visual aid.

After I have gripped the club and constructed a proper visual picture of the shot from behind, I step into my address position, using my left foot as a reference point. I always determine the position of the ball by using my leading side, which is the left. Before I have moved my left foot into position I want to make very sure that the clubface is set properly behind the ball, perpendicular to my intended target line. Once the clubface is in position, then I can worry about the exact alignment of my body. I see a lot of players, some very good ones, who step up to the ball with their right foot leading. This, I think, is not as reliable a pattern as one that involves the left foot as a guide. Throughout your golf swing, the left side is the leader. The left arm determines the radius of the swing, and your left side guides the right side into the impact area. So, it seems only a matter of common sense to pay particular heed to the left side when stepping into your address position. With this in mind, I advise you to position your left side first and then allow your right side to follow its lead.

In positioning my body at address, I am apt to favor a setup that has the ball well forward in my stance, particularly with my driver. With my driver and with most of my long clubs, I am looking to sweep the ball toward the target with the sole of the clubhead paralleling the ground at the moment

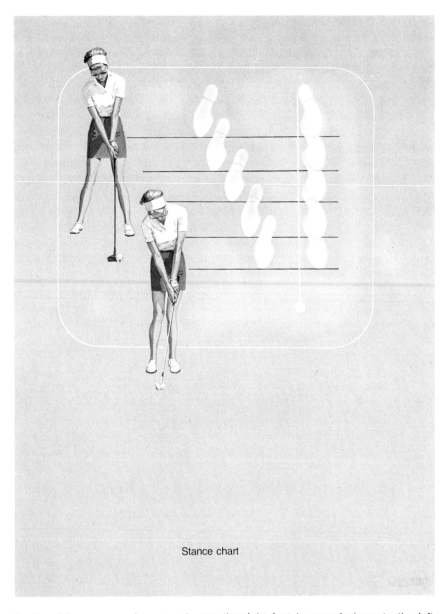

Stance chart

As the club you are using gets shorter, the right foot is moved closer to the left. This may give the illusion that the ball is being moved back in the stance, but in fact its position relative to the left foot and left side of the body never varies. The only possible exceptions occur with the driver, which, because the ball is sitting on a tee, may be played further forward, and when hitting unusual shots, such as the low punch or high lob.

of impact. My reasoning is fairly simple on this point. You are looking to impart the greatest amount of energy to the golf ball, and that energy is best used if it is directed along a line straight toward your target. The best way you can accomplish this is to sweep your clubhead right along the ground through impact and then out toward the target. With the shorter clubs, precision becomes the most important element of the shot. As the length of the club decreases, you will naturally bend more at address and as a result the swing will be more upright, encouraging a down-and-through striking action.

As you move from one club to another, there is no real reason to alter your position. The driver may be played a bit further forward, but remember that the ball is on a tee in that instance. The more often you hit the ball from the same position, the more familiar you are apt to become with your own swing pattern, and the better the chance of that swing repeating each time.

When I am playing a shot with my driver, I tend to position the ball opposite my left instep, almost up to my left toe. This makes it very natural for me to sweep the ball from the tee and allows me to stay well "behind" through impact. I feel that I am trying to strike the back of the ball—more on that later. For medium and even short irons, I never move the ball more than a hair further back than the inside edge of my left heel unless I am trying to hit a special type of shot. When I am swinging properly, I find that the low point in my swing arc falls naturally in a position opposite the inside edge of my left shoulder. This corresponds with a point almost exactly opposite the inside of my left heel. It is the point at which I want to make contact with the ball. With the shorter clubs, the ball positioned to the right of my left heel, the more upright path allows me to strike the ball a bit before the exact bottom of my arc to promote a down-and-through action.

A point of much confusion among weekend golfers involves the orientation of the feet in relation to the alignment of the body. Many teaching professionals advocate having the right foot exactly perpendicular to the target line, with the left foot turned about 45° out toward the target. I have found that there is no one set prescription for positioning the feet—it depends on the individual. If you find that you are having trouble making a good full turn away from the ball, you might try turning your right foot out (away from the target) and turning your left foot back toward a more perpendicular position. If, on the other hand, you are making a good backswing turn but are having trouble returning powerfully to the ball, it would be worth your while to turn only your left foot more toward the target. This will promote freedom of motion through the ball.

Because the main point of this book is to teach you to swing in as natural a fashion as possible, I want to have you stand up to the ball in a comfortable posture. With this in mind, you should assume an address position that allows you to stand with your left arm comfortably extended, your knees slightly flexed, and your right arm and side set down and back. The right side should feel passive, the left active. There is a certain amount of bending at the hip joints and your weight is more toward the middle of your feet —never on your toes! The extension of the left arm and the relaxation of the right will promote a swinging action that is controlled mostly by the left side. The flex in your knees will allow your legs to work smoothly and powerfully throughout the swing. The overall sensation at address should be one of readiness and stability, with the left side in a position of control. Because the right hand sits further down the shaft than the left, the entire right side of the body must be lower than the left. This is a very important point, but not one that you should overexaggerate. If you allow your right side to relax naturally from the outset, it will automatically be lower than your left. It is a simple physical fact. If you find that your right side is too high at address with the arm fully extended, you are probably standing too far from the ball. Also, if your right hand is in too weak a position on the club, too far over the top of the grip, then your entire right side will be pulled up and around. I think that the key word in this whole matter of positioning the two sides of your body is "extended." At address, the left arm is extended and the right arm is not. If the right arm is extended there is a flaw somewhere.

The feeling promoted by a proper address position is one of being set well behind the ball, with room enough to work your weight toward the target through impact. You should feel balanced and very solidly set on both feet. Your knees will be comfortably flexed, and you will bend over slightly from the hip joints.

When I was first learning the basics of the game, setting up behind the ball was something that came very easily to me. In fact, when I grew strong enough to begin taking a divot with my irons, I found that my emphasis on being behind the ball gave my swing such a sweeping action at impact that I was actually unable to strike down into the ground. After a little while I adjusted my address position slightly, but I still set up well behind the ball. It is for this reason that I have never had a problem with "coming over the top of the swing"—swinging down and across the ball rather than out through it. The feeling of being behind the ball also encourages strong use of the legs and a good, free extension through impact.

Once you have established a comfortable relationship between your body and the ball, your next step is to position your body with respect to your intended target. The manner in which you align your body with respect

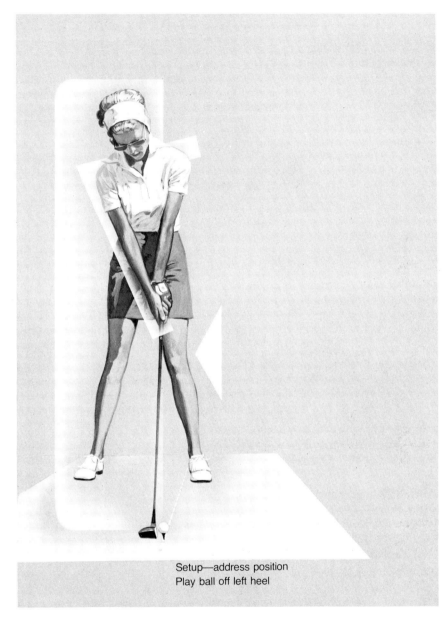

Setup—address position
Play ball off left heel

At address, the right side is down and relaxed, ready to follow the guide of the left side. The right shoulder is lowered to allow the right hand to sit below the left on the grip. A comfortable flex in the knees allows the lower body to feel alive and ready for action. The body is set well behind the ball to allow full utilization of available power at impact.

to the target is perhaps the most important factor involved in the execution of the successful golf shot.

For the average player, important alignment is probably the most common major swing flaw. Also, happily, it is the easiest to correct. Proper alignment is a matter of static positioning; it requires no intricate movement of the body and no physical abilities beyond the ability to stand in a particular position, pointing in a particular direction.

It is because alignment is such an important factor in my golf game that I take particular care to approach each shot from behind so that I can get a clear visual image of the intended line from my ball to the target.

Throughout this chapter, reference will be made to "the target line." The target line is simply an imaginary line extending from your ball to your target. When I refer to "swing line," I am speaking of a line described by your clubhead as it moved through the impact area. These two lines, the target line and the swing line, combined with the position of your clubface at impact, constitute the only variables affecting the flight and destination of your golf ball. Ideally, you are looking for a golf swing and an alignment pattern that will allow your swing to coincide exactly with your target line at impact, with the face of your club exactly perpendicular to these lines at the moment the ball is taken, and the clubhead releasing out toward the target. In other words, you are looking to establish parallels, with everything moving in one direction. If you can actually accomplish this, you will, in theory, hit a straight shot that is dead on line toward your target.

One of the simpler facts about the way your body reacts during the golf swing is often overlooked by the average weekend player.

The next time you have the opportunity to study sequence photographs of a good golfer in action, notice that the line of his clubhead through impact, or the swing line, almost always parallels the line set by the shoulders and upper body at address. In other words, if your shoulders are set exactly parallel to your intended target line at address, the physical tendency will be for your hands to return the clubhead along a line that coincides with that target line, through impact.

The position of your feet and legs at address is important and your shoulders and upper body should follow the pattern set by your feet.

Of course, common sense would indicate that if you allow your shoulders and upper body to become radically out of line with your feet and lower body, you will be unable to coordinate properly the movements of the upper and lower parts of your body. For the average player, the best policy is always to align yourself so that a line across your feet and the line of your shoulders are pointing in the same direction. If you don't manipulate each part of your body, it will fall into place fairly easily. Alignment of your hips

Lining up

When lining up, pick a distinct spot in your target area, then envision a straight line running from that spot to your position. After setting up this line, make certain that your feet, hips and shoulders are aligned parallel to it, with the face of the club exactly perpendicular to your intended target.

and shoulders is a good thing to check occasionally. This will make the task of aligning your upper body much simpler since you can begin the process by correctly setting your feet parallel to the intended target line. Then you can worry about making certain that your body is set in such a fashion that allows the shoulders, hips and feet to point in the same direction.

When the average player hears someone speak of a "closed" or "open" stance, he or she has no real knowledge of what exactly is meant by each of those terms. The closing or opening of your stance involves more than the simple advancement or withdrawal of one of your feet with respect to the target line. Simply pulling your left foot back away from the target line does not put you in a proper open stance. As mentioned earlier in this section, the line of your clubhead through impact tends to follow the line established by your shoulders at address and not that established by your lower body, assuming that the lower and upper portions of your body are aligned in two different directions. Therefore any adjustments in stance must be made with more than just the lower body, since it is actually the upper body that determines the path of your swing and thus the flight of your shot.

To open or close your stance correctly, it is necessary that you align your entire body to one side of the target line. For a proper open stance, you should be aligned as though you wished to hit a straight shot to a point left of your actual target. Because the clubface is aimed at your real target, it will be open with respect to the swing line encouraged by your alignment pattern. The shot will start toward your imaginary target and curve to the right in flight. The same theory applies to a closed stance, although in that case you will be aligned toward a point to the right of your actual target.

The term "alignment" refers not only to the direction in which your body is facing, but also to the coordination at address between the various portions of your body. Again, for the weekend player, it is a good idea to concentrate on aligning yourself so that your feet, legs, hips, upper body and shoulders are all parallel to the same line. You may hear, from time to time, that several of the stronger male touring pros set up slightly open to the ball, even for straight shots. This is fine if you are strong enough through the hands and forearms to be able to afford a restricted movement in your hips and lower body. For most of us, it is absolutely necessary that we get a full and complete turn, so that we can put each and every muscle in our bodies to efficient use. Swing restriction is a luxury that few, very practiced, strong people can afford to incorporate into their golf swings.

6

The Backswing:
Priming the Body

Everything that I do during my backswing is designed to allow me to make most efficient use of every muscle in my body. Proper use of legs, hips, shoulders, arms and hands is an absolute must if a person of my size is to generate enough power to play competitive golf. The plane of my backswing is, in classic instructional terms, a fairly flat plane, meaning that I swing the club around more behind my head than above my head. This plane has me arriving at the top of my backswing with my hands very close to the level of my right shoulder. The player with a more upright plane, though, would have his hands a good six to eight inches above the right shoulder, and perhaps more in extreme cases.

I feel that the flat swing provides the most natural method of striking a golf ball. I feel as though I am able to create more club speed when swinging on a flatter plane, because the movements throughout my entire body are better coordinated. It becomes very unnatural for me to attempt to swing the club on an upright plane and still try to get a full turn through the body, because it does not seem that everything is working together.

If you were to stand in a natural address position, without a golf club in your hand and with your left arm extended, and then if you swing your left arm around your body without making any unnatural or forced move to position the arm above your shoulders, you would find that the arm just naturally wheels back on a fairly flat plane. To move it on an upright plane it seems as though there has to be a separate, unnatural move, a lifting action in the arms and hands somewhere midway through the backswing.

To allow the club to do anything other than revolve around and go behind my head is to create an additional unnecessary movement.

To coordinate the movements of the hands and body most effectively, I think that the hands should be kept swinging on a plane as close to the plane of the shoulder-turn as possible, and that means a fairly flat swing plane.

I'm certain that some of you will be up in arms at this point if you have watched players like JoAnne Carner, Johnny Miller, and Jack Nicklaus who swing the clubhead and their hands on a relatively upright plane, high above their right shoulder at the top of the swing. What you have to understand in these instances is that these are very strong, very practiced players, with tremendous feel, who can afford to sacrifice a bit of pure power. Anyone with a much better than average amount of strength is naturally going to be able to get away with a few things that the normal person simply cannot. This is one of the big inequities between men's professional golf and women's. Most of the male touring pros can afford to restrict and confine their swings for the sake of accuracy and consistency, whereas the majority of players on the LPGA tour need to make full use of *all* of their strength and physical coordination for the sake of power. Their first concern is achieving sufficient distance to reach greens in regulation figures. A man can naturally get away with certain flaws that a woman cannot, simply because in women's golf there is no room for error. A male touring pro might hit a drive off of the neck of his club, or sky a ball off the tee, and in most cases all this will mean is that he will be forced to hit a 7-iron rather than a 9-iron into a par 4 hole.

If someone on the LPGA tour makes the same mistake with the driver, chances are that she will not even be able to reach the green of a par 4 with a 3-wood, since under normal circumstances most of our par 4s are at least a driver and a long iron. Remember that striving for power with a game like my own does not mean that I can give up any accuracy. My margin of error is not nearly as great as that of a good male golfer because of the strength factor. In other words, while hitting the ball my maximum distance, I must also keep it in play.

So, for women professionals and most weekend players, both men and women, it becomes very important to eliminate as many mistakes as you can. Of course you can never eliminate all of them, but you must strive to build a swing that is as natural as possible and is thus very easy to keep in good repair.

Another advantage of swinging on a fairly flat plane is that a flat swing will naturally bring your hands more inside the line, allowing you to swing the clubhead out toward the target more easily. Anyone who is looking for a few extra yards off the tee must realize that a shot that moves from right to left (for a right-handed golfer) will travel a good deal further than a faded

Sequence *(cont'd)*

Here you can readily appreciate the differences between a very upright swing, such as JoAnne Carner's, and the flatter-planed, fuller swing that I use and teach. With a more generous turn throughout the body, I am able to position the club further inside the intended swing line at the top of my backswing. From this position I am able to return the clubhead to the ball from the inside with relative ease. Aside from the accuracy developed by my method, the full backswing turn that you see in my swing allows me to move my entire body through the ball at impact, generating maximum speed and power.

or sliced shot. Again, anyone who can afford the luxury of fading the ball consistently must be a person of above-average strength who has no worries about achieving sufficient length. When I find it necessary to fade or cut the ball into a green, I always take one more club. JoAnne Carner, for instance, plays the ball from left to right almost exclusively. JoAnne is, however, an exceptionally strong player and can afford this sort of sacrifice. In fact, JoAnne's swing exhibits many of the restrictions that a strong, talented player can afford to incorporate, but that an average player must stay away from.

Some people feel that an upright swing is a bit more accurate, because the club stays closer to the intended swing line throughout the entire swing. But an upright plane discourages a good turn and, as a result, costs many of us a great deal of clubhead speed. Also, amateurs invariably have the most problems with swinging from the outside across the ball. I feel, though, that with my grip and my method of swinging the club, the golfer is able to make a more powerful and more accurate pass at the ball, because the clubhead is moving toward the target for a greater length of time without the hands rotating, and the player is encouraged to be behind the ball and driving through impact with the lower body.

The well-synchronized action that is encouraged by swinging on a fairly flat plane is only possible if the motions of your body away from the ball are well coordinated and made in one piece. In saying "one piece," I mean that the hands, the clubhead, your upper and lower body all begin to leave the ball at the same time.

Some people find it easier to begin this one-piece motion if they use a slight forward press at the outset, meaning they move their hands or their right knee slightly toward the target and then begin the backswing almost as a recoil action. I do this myself at times. The point is that everything is encouraged to leave the ball at once.

I don't think that there is one particular part of the body that initiates the entire motion. I think the forward press is, for many people, advantageous just as a means of setting the entire body in motion, so that the first move from the ball may be smooth and well-knit. Everything leaves together and, I believe, everything stays together up to a point—approximately midway through the backswing—where the weight of the clubhead causes the wrists to begin cocking naturally. Starting away from the ball in one piece and turning there should be a constant emphasis on full extension with the left arm creating as big an arc as possible.

For me the cocking of the wrists is a very natural, gradual movement that requires no specific thought and no abrupt action. At that certain point in the swing, the extended weight of the clubhead simply becomes too great

Sequence *(cont'd)*

Two of the most important characteristics of the backswing are extension and turn. The weight must be turned to the right side during the backswing, and the left side of the body must extend fully if the swing is to have sufficient width. When working on your backswing, these two thoughts—extension and turn—should be kept in mind as keys.

for your hands to control without trying to work underneath the grip so that they can better support this weight. As the hands begin cocking, they begin moving underneath the grip. The whole motion is very smooth and very natural.

I won't say that the wrist break begins at exactly the same place for every player. However, all of those players who make a good one-piece movement from the ball seem to begin to cock their wrists approximately at the same point in the swing. People who break their wrists very early are not making a natural move at all. Breaking your wrists very early is a forced move, done intentionally and with conscious thought.

As your backswing begins to gather momentum, it is very natural for the bulk of your body weight to move onto your right side. A good thought to keep in mind at this stage of the swing is to *turn* your weight to the right. The traditional phrase, "shift your weight to the right," almost suggests lateral motion, which is something you do not want during your backswing. It is a turning motion.

As the backswing approaches the top, the majority of your weight should be settled solidly on your right heel. I think that the biggest mistake the average player could make at this stage would be to attempt to restrict the flow of weight to the right side. There are people who play this way and play well. But it requires an awful lot of very quick movement and a tremendous amount of strength and agility in the legs. To my mind it's a lot of wasted energy.

Once you have the sense of turning the weight smoothly to your right heel and then throughout the entire right side of your body, then you can take every ounce that you have and put it solidly into the ball.

Proper windup during the backswing prepares you for a quick and efficient transfer of weight through impact and allows you to generate a maximum of useful power. In most cases, a full windup necessitates raising your left heel to some extent. If you feel the heel rise toward the top of the backswing, let it go. The only restricting factor during your backswing should be balance. You should strive to make as large a turn throughout your entire body as is possible without pulling your head off the ball or allowing your weight to move past the point of good balance. Beyond these requirements, I feel that nothing should limit the degree of turn that you strive for during the backswing. Whenever I want to drive the ball particularly far, I try to feel a greater coil and fuller turn throughout my body.

In recent years it has become fashionable to speak of many sorts of restriction in the backswing. One of the terms that is used most frequently and is least understood by the amateur golfer is the phrase "hip restriction." I think that this phrase has done an almost unbelievable amount of

Sequence *(cont'd)*

When I refer to a turn during the backswing, I mean exactly that. The proper backswing is not a lift or a slide, but a full, gradual turn of the entire body away from the ball. As a checkpoint in determining whether you have made a full turn during the backswing, make certain that you feel the bulk of your weight planted solidly on your right heel after you've completed your backswing.

harm to more golfers than I would care to count. If your weight is kept solidly on the heel of your right foot at the top of your backswing, your hips can be turned to their maximum degree with no fear of overturning or disrupting your swing plane. In fact, most amateur golfers who consciously restrict the turning motion of their hips prevent their hands from ever swinging properly to the inside during the backswing. They set themselves up to be ahead of the swing and over the top with the upper body. Coming through the ball, their right hips jut out into the hitting area, blocking any powerful hand action and causing their hands to pull across the ball. That produces a slice.

If you look at photographs of a good professional golfer, you will notice that his or her hips are turned at least 45° from the ball in the backswing. My own hips are turned almost completely away from my target at the completion of the backswing for a full shot.

For the amateur player who is probably attempting to get rid of a chronic slice, the hips should turn to an even greater degree, allowing the entire right side of the body to move back from the target line, leaving the hands a clear path on the inside from which they can approach the ball.

If a golfer will just learn to get the club moving low along the ground at the beginning of his or her backswing, with all parts of the body together, and then make one continuous movement from that point, letting the motion carry the swing to the top, there is very little that can be wrong with the backswing.

Once you begin thinking consciously of positions, restrictions and artificial planes, you limit the continuity of that motion and the backswing becomes a disjointed action guaranteed to destroy almost all chance of proper timing and coordination through impact.

If you will just erase from your mind all the preconceptions that you have acquired about the swing and attempt to build a smooth, sweeping, one-piece backswing, you will be well along the way to developing a natural power swing.

7

The Downswing: Letting It Go

At the top of your backswing, you are coiled and ready to move, but not tense or tight. From this wound-up position the first move needed for a proper downswing is one that will set the lower body ahead of the upper body. Replacing the weight upon the left foot accomplishes this purpose. It begins the motion in the lower part of your body and the shifting of the weight to the left, and initiates the driving action of your legs so important to the achievement of power and consistency. Your hips begin coming back to the square position that they started from and, without any conscious thought, this move allows your hands to drop to a proper inside track, and to keep the upper body behind the ball at impact.

As I begin to start down, I am not particularly conscious of any one part of my body. Rather, my thoughts are on hitting the golf ball flush, then extending the club through the ball toward the target. As a result, the path of the downswing more or less takes care of itself. Because there is one direct route from the top to the ball that the hands will follow naturally if given the chance.

So long as the legs and lower body are used to begin the downswing, the hands will not, generally, be able to move out of the swing plane. If you make a good initial move, you will only be able to disrupt the swing by consciously adding something to it.

During the periods of my career when I was particularly distance-conscious, I kept reminding myself of the importance of the legs in achieving power. Bob Toski had taught me how good foot- and legwork would develop clubhead speed. I was very aware of the lateral motion in the knees at the beginning of the downswing, and of the correct placement and

Sequence *(cont'd)*

Remember that all of the movement of the downswing is initiated by the motion of the lower body toward the target. When the legs move first, the hands are automatically pulled down into a proper slot and the upper body is kept behind the ball, from where it can deliver full power at the ball.

transfer of weight throughout the downswing, particularly during impact.

Nowadays, when I feel as though I'm not hitting the ball quite as hard as I can, I go back to thinking about the correct transfer of weight and the power that is available from good movement in the legs.

The legs and hips are important in generating power; they are also responsible for the shape of the swing through impact, which is, to my way of thinking, one of the most important characteristics of any golf swing.

As you begin moving from the top of your backswing through the ball, your knees will naturally have to drive toward the left in a lateral motion. What this does is tend to level off the arc of the downswing through the hitting area, giving you a wider range in which accurate contact may be made. If you were to develop a golf swing that was perfectly circular, the effective impact area of, as I refer to it, the flat area at the bottom of the swing would be no more than an inch or two in length. The club would come to and leave the line very quickly. By utilizing leg-drive through impact, you are able to convert a circular motion into a flatter, more elliptical arc as you pass through the hitting area, and thus allow the clubhead to stay on the intended line of flight for a much longer period. In this fashion, the legs at once add both power and accuracy to the swing.

If you watch a player like Lee Trevino, you will notice that one of the biggest assets to his golf swing is the effective size of his impact area. Trevino's great lateral motion in his legs and lower body allows him to keep the clubhead swinging down the line for perhaps eight or twelve inches, and provides him with a tremendous area in which precise contact may be made. His hands and the clubhead are moving through the ball and toward the target for an awfully long time. This is probably why he is one of the most accurate strikers of the ball ever to play the game. Jack Nicklaus's lateral move and long hitting area are also very evident, though not as pronounced as Trevino's.

Something that I notice from time to time is the absence of this lateral move and long hitting area in many women players. And I don't understand exactly why this is, because the woman golfer needs the benefit of every possible advance in technique to compensate for her lack of strength.

Proper utilization of the legs and a long drive through the hitting area make me able to hit the ball up alongside people who should be much longer than I am. I take advantage of every little thing that a person can use to develop effective power throughout the golf swing. Proper use of the legs in the downswing serves a dual purpose. The lateral move develops tremendous power because it creates speed and allows you to delay the release of the clubhead. The flattening of the arc through the impact area develops accuracy and precision in striking the ball.

Sequence *(cont'd)*
Comparison at impact

When the legs are allowed to guide the upper body toward impact, the swing levels off in the hitting area, giving the golfer a long, flat zone within which accurate contact can be made. All golfers with strong lower-body action, like myself and Lee Trevino, are able to keep the clubhead moving toward the target for a long time, making it simpler to hit straight shots.

The longer the clubhead can travel toward the target, the longer the ball will travel straight. The possibility of putting any spin on the ball is greatly lessened if the clubhead does not deviate from the intended line of flight for a good three to four inches after the ball is struck. Any time the clubhead is moving rapidly across the line in either direction at the moment of impact, your chances of putting some sort of sidespin on the ball are greatly increased.

As I approach the impact area, I feel that my only task is to allow the complete release of all the speed and power that have been built up in my body by the rest of my golf swing.

Up until this point, I have been very concerned with turning, coiling, extending, transferring my weight and, in general, putting myself into the most powerful position possible. The last few feet of the swing, however, are simply a result of all this motion. And the player—he or she—is much better off just to let this happen. You should be very very conscious of letting everything go through impact, not trying to restrain any of the natural motion or clubhead speed that has been developed up to this point. A very great fault among people who sometimes hit the ball well but are often inconsistent is stopping the clubhead or slowing it down through impact. They hit the ball and think, "Well, that's it." A scientist could probably tell you that if you stop the club just past impact, you have begun the slowing-down process sometime long before the actual striking of the ball, which means that you have lost a good deal of your effective power.

That's why people have to learn to let the entire swing go at and through impact. For the most part, it is a matter of convincing yourself that the clubhead is in the proper path and can do the job without any further conscious direction. If the club is not allowed to swing freely through impact, your clubhead speed is not going to be as great, and consequently your length and accuracy will suffer.

At impact and through the ball, the palm of your right hand should feel as though it's been pulled out along the line toward the target. It's almost as if the palm of your right hand represented the clubface. The right hand drives down the line squarely toward the intended target, and the clubhead follows.

The action of the right hand through impact is fairly important in terms of the amount of power you are able to generate. There should be no conscious effort to whip the right hand through the ball. Nevertheless, proper action in the legs and through the left side gives you the feeling that the right hand is releasing powerfully through impact, with no effort on your part.

At a very early stage in my golfing career, I was taught to swing the club out to the right after impact. I don't think that the club actually goes out to the right after the ball has been struck, but the feeling that you are extending it away from your body helps promote good extension past the ball and maximum clubhead speed through impact.

It seems to me that in the golf swing you have to exaggerate everything a bit in order to get into the proper position. So while my effort was expended in learning to swing the club to the right, I was in fact learning how to swing the club out toward the target, right along the line.

So many weekend players, feeling as though they must control the club to a great degree during impact, restrict the natural extension of the arms and the clubhead after the ball has been struck, often pulling their hands in toward their body, cutting across the face of the ball and causing a weak slice. The simple effort to allow the hands and clubhead to swing out well away from the body toward the target, until the arms have reached their maximum degree of extension, will do much to eliminate the weekend player's chronic lack of power and consistency.

One aspect of my golf swing that I was not actually taught was the followthrough. I think that my finish position is actually a result of my trying to swing the club out to the right beyond impact. I can't really say that I can feel where the clubhead is moving two or three feet after impact. Once I feel that my hands and arms are at their maximum extension point, I am not particularly aware of the followthrough. I think that this is a good thing, because by not consciously directing my followthrough I'm making sure that it is simply a reaction to the speed that has been built up during my swing. The extension that takes place beyond impact is not quite the same as the extension that takes place during the first few feet of your backswing. There is really very little momentum acting to pull your swing through into the proper positions during your backswing. Beyond the ball, though, there is a tremendous amount of speed and momentum developed in your clubhead. And it is this speed, produced through impact, that forces you into the proper followthrough position.

A few feet beyond impact, your body has to begin to turn away from the line of flight and then the club goes on to a finish. You are not actually swinging the club to a finish. You are simply holding on to it and allowing it to spend the tremendous momentum that has been built up. If you force the club to an unnaturally high position or to an unnaturally full followthrough position, you are indicating that the clubhead speed developed through impact was insufficient to bring your swing to a proper conclusion.

The only place that you need to go in the followthrough is as far as your club will take you. The whole point of the impact area and beyond is a complete letting-go, allowing everything to move according to the dictates of the swinging action that has been built up. A natural followthrough is simply the result of a good, unconscious, free release of your full power through impact. Your hands will naturally finish a little higher above your left shoulder during the followthrough than they were over your right shoulder at the top of your backswing because your body is arched at the end of the followthrough and you've swung the clubhead out toward the target, whereas at the top of your backswing this was not the case.

For most men and women golfers, I think that this picture of impact is going to make the whole thing much easier than it would be if they tried to restrict their turn, or hit against a solid left side, or take the club from a square-to-square position. These are all very difficult things that can hardly be understood by the playing professional, much less the weekend amateur. I just don't think that the average player, who gets out on a golf course once or twice a week, is going to be able to incorporate these complicated positions into a golf swing.

I think that I could help ninety per cent of the male golfers at any country club simply by teaching them to get their left arm and left side well extended during the entire swing. The left arm finally relaxes and folds, going to the follow through. These tips will help people very quickly without their having to spend weeks on the practice range. The simple change in the left-hand position will bring good results in little time. Most male golfers have left-hand grips that are so weak (and the hand is weak anyway), that it's nearly impossible for them to coordinate the motions of the two sides of their body properly during the swing.

Now, without dismantling their golf swings and starting from scratch, I could give them just a few small tips that would really help to get them into better position from start to finish.

To begin with, just a minor grip change throws you into the desirable positions that people have been striving for for a long time and have never achieved. The strong left-hand grip tends to keep your entire body behind the ball through impact, which is one of the real keys to long driving. The heel of your left hand is a very natural leader during the downswing and if you allow it to direct your hands and arms and clubhead into the ball, the chronic fault of hitting early with the right side, of pushing the entire right side over the top of the swing plane, will be eliminated.

Because the heel of the left hand seems much more natural a leader than the back of the left hand, people will be encouraged to allow the left hand and arm to dominate properly the upper body motion from the top of the swing into the ball. This, combined with good movement in the legs, will really encourage a nice, powerful release through impact and total utilization of whatever strength the player has.

Sequence *(cont'd)*

With the left-hand grip that I teach, the heel of the left hand becomes a natural leader during the downswing. If the heel of the left hand leads the clubhead to the ball, the face of the club will be kept looking down the intended target line—before, through, and after impact.

Until now I have not made any specific reference to the importance of head positioning during your golf swing. I don't think that it is possible for anyone who plays golf these days to be unaware of the importance of a steady head in controlling the entire pattern of a golf swing. Endless pages have been devoted to this topic and I think that this is just as it should be. Head position is really one of the most important things you can concern yourself with in building a golf game.

I don't think that any amateur golfer can spend too much time learning to keep his swing firmly anchored and his head solidly in place. I recall hearing somewhere that Arnold Palmer spent an entire year working on head position. That should be enough to recommend this sort of effort to any golfer.

Without a steady head it is almost impossible to generate maximum power through impact. In fact, allowing the head to move forward as the downswing progresses is one of the most destructive practices evident in the games of most weekend players.

As soon as your head moves forward, ahead of its original address position during the downswing, the bulk of your weight will have been forced beyond the ball before it has been given any chance to be used through impact. Thus, with your head out in front of the proper position, you will be reduced to flailing at the ball with your hands and arms, since all of the natural strength in the large muscles in your back and legs will be unavailable through the impact area. In addition, when the head is allowed to move forward as the ball is struck, the upper body tends to move beyond its original position far too quickly and the hands are never able to catch up. There is no release of the hands through impact, and a weak, sliced shot is generally the result.

Aside from keeping your head fixed behind the ball through the downswing, it is important that you prevent your head from turning until well after the ball has been struck. If the head turns toward the target prematurely, the entire right side of the body will tend to rise and come around the ball rather than under and through it. This is why you will often see good players cock their heads slightly away from the target before beginning their swing. This makes them very conscious of preventing any head movement, either lateral or rotary, as the ball is being taken. My own head is cocked slightly behind the ball at address and throughout the swing.

One of the very common instructional concepts that is seldom understood by the average player is the idea of releasing the hands through impact. In the traditional swing style there is some rotation of the hands and arms as the club is taken away on the backswing, and there is similar rotation of the hands and arms during the downswing, allowing the club to return to the ball in a square position. What happens, in effect, is that the club opens going away from the ball and then closes coming into the ball.

The strong left-hand grip that I preach allows you to eliminate this movement both on the backswing and on the downswing. With the strong left-hand grip you will find that you don't need to make any conscious rolling motion of the hands and arms through impact to bring the club to a square position. Your hands will probably respond more naturally through impact, and you will find a comfortable release.

With the heel of the left hand leading to the ball, the wrists can uncock naturally, with no conscious effort to manipulate the club into a square position through the hitting area.

With my swing method, the term "release" is simply a reference to the unleashing of all the power that has been built up by the backswing coil and the natural cocking of the wrists. To go back to the analogy of the hammer, when I speak of release I am merely speaking of the same motion that is used in the wrist when driving a nail with a hammer. That is, the natural uncocking that occurs as the heel of the hand leads the hammer to its target. At some point after impact the hands will naturally roll over, as the right hand and arm reach their point of maximum extension. With my swing, this happens not prior to impact but well after the ball has begun its flight. And thus the turning over of the hands in no way affects the eventual success of the shot.

Because the hands do not roll over to the left nearly as quickly with my style, the player is encouraged to keep the clubhead moving down the intended line for a much longer period of time. This gets back to the concept of a long impact area which I discussed earlier in this chapter, and it is one of the most natural and beneficial results of my swing method.

At this point, I will try and outline some of the desired feelings that one should have through the downswing and into the followthrough. From the coiled position at the top of the backswing, the golfer's first move involves the lowering of the left heel and, simultaneously, the driving of the legs laterally toward the target. This motion to the left naturally forces your hands and arms to drop down and to the inside. At this point you should feel as though your hands are well behind your body and well inside the intended swing line. Once the shift of weight to the left and the driving of the legs has put your hands into a properly lowered position with your upper body behind your lower body, your sole thought should be to release through the ball, keeping your head fixed firmly behind and then extending your hands and arms out toward the target. You should feel as though you are leading with the heel of your left hand directly to the ball. This will eliminate any conscious thought of downswing plane or clubhead path through impact. Simply concentrate on a solid hit and as you approach the ball you must convince yourself to let everything go, with your hands, the clubhead and the golf ball flying out toward the target, propelled by the momentum that has been created by your golf swing. From there, if you have let everything release through impact, you will find yourself turning naturally to a balanced, well-extended finish.

Sequence *(cont'd)*

If you allow your swing to release fully through impact, the momentum of the swing-ing clubhead will naturally bring your hands into a high, fully extended finish position.

8

Tempo

One of the most important aspects of any player's game is tempo, meaning the overall speed of the swing motion. Although tempo is really one of the absolute musts in the formation of a successful swing, there is no one set tempo that is right for everyone. Every person has a natural tempo that is uniquely his/her own. Whatever that tempo is—slow, fast, or in-between—the key to making it a successful contributor to your golf swing is learning to make it the same, day in and day out. This will take most of the ups and downs out of your golf game, because consistent tempo naturally brings on consistent timing, and timing is one of the variables upon which your game rides from day to day. Years ago when I was playing a lot of golf with Bob Toski, Bob's great rhythm and tempo rubbed off on me. My swing got smoother just from observing his.

I suppose that Julius Boros is everybody's classic example of a golfer with a good tempo. The overall pace of his swing rarely changes. And that is why Julius looks as though he is swinging in exactly the same way every time you see him play. On our tour, Mary Mills is the finest example of a golfer with good rhythm and tempo, both in smoothness and consistency. I would say that Arnold Palmer, on the other hand, is the sort of golfer who has a fairly erratic tempo. And I think that perhaps is why, even though Arnold is a great player, he's had his ups and downs throughout his career. It seems as though he is either perfectly timed and perfectly in control of his whole swing or struggling a bit to keep everything in tune.

There are certain parts of your game in which tempo is a much more important factor. I think that all good wedge players are people with beautiful, smooth tempos. The best I can do in describing it would be to call it a fluid motion, which seems to me to be one of the absolute keys to being a good wedge player, and I've yet to see a golfer who had this ability—to hit wonderfully smooth wedge shots—come up with very many tempo problems.

For the most part, tempo is smoothness, but beyond that, tempo is also a generation of speed. For instance, a player who leaves the ball very deliberately and then all of a sudden attempts to speed up his swing in order to get more power is not swinging with any sort of tempo. It is all a forced action. But then, there are players who leave the ball rather deliberately and the pace of their swing gradually increases until they are accelerating very smoothly and very powerfully through the ball. And that is their particular, very individual tempo, and it is something easily repeated.

One thing that people do not really understand is that you can go out on the golf course with basically the same golf swing two or three days in a row, but if the tempo has gone wrong, your timing goes, the rhythm goes, the coordination goes. Then everything is gone.

One example of this that comes quickly to mind is Mickey Wright. Mickey has one of the greatest golf swings in the world, and the basic positions of that swing never change from day to day. But she hits the ball poorly when her tempo is off, when the motions of her swing are not properly paced and coordinated. Tempo is really the only problem that ever arises in her game.

One of the very important things about a consistent rhythm and tempo is that it will allow you to get away with many small swing mistakes from time to time. Good tempo makes it difficult for any one part of the swing to get too far out of joint. And thus you are probably not going to hit too many horrible shots, even when you're not swinging as well as you'd like. Since we are all human, we are all going to show small flaws from day to day. And good tempo is one of the practical methods of trying to play in spite of them.

One important caution here is that you not try to pattern your tempo after another player. Just because you see Jack Nicklaus start for the ball very deliberately, or because you see Arnold Palmer move very quickly into his backswing, doesn't mean that either one of these tempos will suit your particular game.

Tempo varies from person to person, and it's no more than the natural speed at which you'd do anything. Some people dress very quickly, and for some people it takes an awfully long time. The tempo that is right for you in swinging a golf club depends pretty much on the type of person you are. If you are a person who tends to speak very quickly, walk fast and, in general do things with greater speed than most, and you go out on the golf course and attempt to swing as deliberately as Jack Nicklaus, then you'll be basing your swing on an unnatural rhythm and tempo. And your chances for successful golf will be slim.

I've always been a little on the quick side as far as my golf swing is concerned. That's something I recognize and accept. When I'm playing well, that tempo works very well for me. And it really would hurt my golf game an awful lot if I were to try and slow it down deliberately. So it's very important to be conscious of your own natural swing speed. In fact, it's something that you should try and find during your practice sessions and then stick with.

The key to a successful tempo is that it feels natural and easy to repeat. If I had to generalize, I would say that where tempo is concerned, most weekend players are inclined to be too fast rather than too slow. This is due largely to the fact that they never allow themselves to extend their muscles fully during the backswing. And thus there isn't sufficient motion to slow them down as they take the club to the top.

When I find I'm too quick at the top of my swing, the simple thought of extending the club and my left side makes me slow down with no conscious effort. By concentrating on extension I make my arc a bit bigger, make my turn fuller and the whole action takes a bit more time to complete. Thus the moves at the top of my swing are made more slowly and with a more deliberate tempo. Rather than telling a golfer to slow down, which often paralyzes him, I'd say, "Concentrate on making a good, full sweeping turn." Just thinking of that basic, smooth one-piece takeaway will often slow down a player's tempo. It's the poor takeaway that makes for a lot of quick, jerky movements. You've heard all sorts of players complaining about snatching the club away from the ball. All that is the result of a poor takeaway, and there is nothing that can throw off your tempo as quickly as a fast, uncoordinated move away from the ball.

Whereas tempo refers to the blend of movement throughout your golf swing, timing refers to the coordination of specific parts of that movement. In other words, if you were to look at your golf swing as a dance movement, tempo would refer to the overall speed of the dance, fast or slow; while timing would refer to the relation between the individual movements of your hands and feet, no matter what pace they were done at. Timing involves trying to put more than one movement together into a single, cohesive motion.

Proper timing is greatly encouraged by a consistent tempo. It will be much easier for you to have specific events take place in proper sequence during the golf swing if you are thoroughly familiar with the pace at which each event occurs. It will not be a difficult thing for you to coordinate the motions of your hands with the motions of your legs if you are thoroughly familiar with the speed at which your hands and legs tend to move during the swing. Timing problems will, more often than not, be manifest in a lack of balance and a feeling of jerkiness throughout your swing. When one part of the body is out of step with the rest, it becomes impossible to derive maximum power from the actions; also, it is very likely that the proper path of the swing will be disrupted.

I think that good timing can be the result of concentration on a number of very simple, very basic, yet very important swing thoughts.

The smooth one-piece takeaway is one of the best. And beyond the takeaway, you should attempt to block any conscious thought of specific parts of your body; rather, try to coordinate a full turn away from the ball, involving everything, and then a full powerful turn to and through impact, with a feeling of leading to and through with your legs and left hand. By not thinking too much about one specific part of your body, you are not likely to throw your swing motion out of line and destroy whatever chances you may have for proper timing.

Because the style of swing that I am trying to teach in this book encourages a very long hitting area that involves no conscious manipulation of the hands, one of the greatest timing problems that you see in most amateur golfers is eliminated.

If you will just think of moving everything together, away from the ball, and then moving everything freely and without conscious manipulation through the ball, any problems that you may have with your timing will be small ones.

III
The
Scoring
Strokes

9

Chipping, Pitching
and Sand Play

The first thing that I look at when I'm faced with a short shot, either a chip or a pitch, is the amount of green I have to work with. The distance between the pin and the near edge of the green is extremely important, because it determines which club I will hit or what sort of a shot I want to use. Of course your lie has a great deal to do with the shot you are able to hit. But on most well-conditioned golf courses, when faced with a shot to a pin which is very close to the near edge of the green, you will want to try to throw the ball up high and with a great deal of spin to stop it quickly. There are situations where, if you are pitching to a very close pin, you can chip and run the ball up the bank of a green, trying to stop it near the flag. But I feel that any time you allow the ball to run over the ground before the green, rather than to land on the green, you are taking a chance with the contours of the ground. Any golf shot will react more consistently if it is landed on the putting surface, rather than allowed to run up toward the green. So I am always looking for the shot that will allow me to land the ball on the green and still get it close to the hole.

The key to success in the short game is feel. A very delicate touch is the most important thing that you can possess if you wish to be a good short-shot player. That's why your short game requires so much practice compared to the rest of your game. To allow myself to make maximum use of the natural feel that I have and the feel that I've developed, I try not to think of anything besides getting the ball to the hole once I have stepped up to a short shot. All of the variables involved in determining the exact character of the shot that you want to use, the club that you want to hit and the kind of swing that you want to make, are taken into account prior to your standing over the shot.

Once you have programmed your mind and come up with the most practical solution to the particular situation you're in, it is very important to allow your natural sensitivity to take over from there and get the ball to the hole. The mechanical adjustments that are necessary for playing short shots are fairly simple. For a pitch or a chip my feet are slightly closer together than for a full shot and my stance is opened up a bit, so that I have the feeling that I'm swinging the club out toward the hole. One very important thing that you should try to do when pitching the ball, with either a wedge or a sand wedge, is avoid letting your hands turn over prior to impact. As soon as your hands begin to turn over, you take loft off the club and tend to produce a lower-flying shot. And the whole reason that you are pitching with a sand wedge or a pitching wedge is to get the ball high up in the air and have it land softly. You should try to develop the feeling of keeping the clubface square to the hole throughout the shot and even up to the end of the short followthrough that is required. In a full shot, the momentum of the club and the full turn of your body cause your hands to turn over sometime after impact. This sort of momentum is not present in a pitch shot, so there is no need to allow your hands to turn over at any point in the swing or the followthrough. The people who are the very best wedge players do this time and time again: hold the clubface square to the target. They will never allow it to turn over.

As mentioned in the chapter on tempo, I believe that tempo is one of the absolute keys to effective wedge play. When you get too quick it is very difficult to keep the clubface square to the target. The natural momentum developed will cause your hands to turn over sometime during the swing, and you are apt to produce a low, driving shot rather than the high, soft shot that you are looking for. A quick, jerky action with the wedge makes it very, very difficult to hold the club through to the target. Strangely enough, a too-quick action through the ball is often the result of an exceedingly slow backswing. If you are overly deliberate, somewhere in the middle of your swing your subconscious mind will react and tell you that there is not going to be sufficient clubhead speed at impact to get the ball to the hole. You'll make a frantic effort to speed up your hands and the clubhead, and generally you will either hit well behind the ball or produce a low driving shot that will run well past the pin. If you try and speed up your hands artificially, they move out in front of the clubhead, reducing the effective loft, causing you to pinch the shot, sending it low with a great deal of spin. In certain circumstances this is a very desirable action. But, when the conditions call for a high, soft wedge pitch, the low driving shot that results when your hand action gets too quick is certainly not going to get the job done. The key to keeping the wedge square to the target is, I believe, a feeling

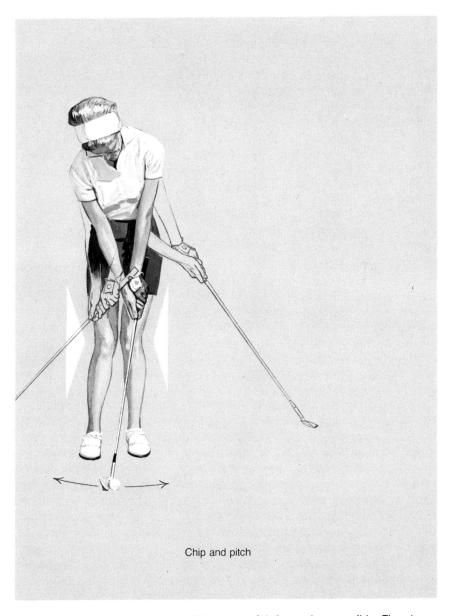

Chip and pitch

For the short shots, the swing should be as straightforward as possible. The stance is slightly open, and the weight is placed on the left foot from the beginning, because there will be little if any transfer of weight during the stroke itself. The hands are ahead, and must lead through the shot with the wrists firm but relaxed. The key to good wedge play is tempo, something that cannot be drawn on this page but must nevertheless be uppermost in your thoughts.

in your left hand and especially in the heel of your left hand of leading the clubhead through to the target. If the left hand stays in a controlling position through impact, there is almost no way that the right hand can climb over the top and take loft off the clubface.

In the short game, just as with full shots, the left side guides the swing and the right hand does help, although the release of the hand Is not conscious and is made only according to the guidelines set forth by the actions of the left hand and the left side of the body. The actual swing for a short pitch shot involves a minimum of body movement and leg movement. The reason for this is that you are really striving for accuracy. Secondly, you are not trying to move the ball any distance. All that you really need to hit a thirty- or forty-yard shot are your hands and arms. Thus any involvement of the body in a pitch shot is really adding unnecessary motion to the swing being used.

In taking the club back, I wouldn't suggest that you try to keep your body stationary. This tends to paralyze you. I would suggest that you try to feel the movement mainly in your arms and hands. The body *will* move slightly in reaction to the motions of your arms and hands. This should not be forced, and certainly should not be overdone. Your knees have to move to provide rhythm and smoothness in the shot. Don't ever, simply for the sake of appearance, force your lower body to move when it is actually unnecessary. The feeling of leading the left hand through impact and holding the face of the wedge open can be promoted by addressing the ball with the hands just a bit in front of the ball. You don't want to move your hands up too far because, again, this will produce a lower shot than you are looking for. But by leading with your hands, say perhaps a half-inch in front of the ball, you put the left side and the left hand in a position of control which is necessary for precise execution.

As you move further and further away from the green, say from fifteen yards to fifty yards, it is necessary to move your feet a little further apart, because as the shot becomes longer, balance is more of a determining factor. To make flush contact with the ball, your balance must be almost perfect in a short shot. With this in mind, you ought to make very certain of placing your feet as far apart as is necessary for you to have a feeling of solidity. From individual to individual this optimum width of stance varies. But I would say, as a general rule, that for a full pitch of seventy to eighty yards, the feet should not be moved more than twelve inches apart at the heels.

A wide stance restricts necessary freedom and forces you to sway off the ball rather than turn. On very little chips or pitches, from twenty yards on in, balance is hardly a factor because there is so little body movement.

Your feet can, in this situation, be very close together, although there is no rule saying they must be. A very narrow stance on short shots is simply a method that has been proven workable by most of golf's best players.

You will see a lot of good players trying to keep the left arm and the club in a straight line through a short chip or a pitch, eliminating any break in the wrist whatsoever. Through the years people have tried to teach me that, but I have found that the one thing you lose with this method is the natural feel and sensitivity that I find so important in making the short shots. I think that it is absolutely imperative that you take advantage of the touch that you have in your hands and fingers, as these are certainly the most sensitive parts of your body involved in making a golf swing. A completely stiff-wristed stroke eliminates the feel in the small sensitive muscles in the hands and fingers, and then feel is no longer an important factor. And I think that most of us can play golf a lot more naturally if we react to our feel rather than to any mechanical precepts. If you do allow your wrists to flex somewhat during a short shot, as I do, it is very important to be in control of them at all times. When I say that I like to see a little wrist break on a pitch shot, I don't mean that I want to see the hands become loose and floppy. I think that a certain amount of break in the wrists helps you to develop a sense of feel. But you should always have control of the clubhead and your hands as they react to movements of the clubhead. It would be totally unnatural to take the club back to a waist-high position needed for a thirty- or forty-yard shot, and then attempt to break the wrists as fully as they are broken on a full swing, for a pitch shot on which you are using about a half-swing. It is natural to allow the wrists to break to about the same degree they would break midway through the backswing in a full shot. So for a half-swing with the wedge, just imagine the position in which you'd find your wrists halfway through the backswing on a full driver shot. This will be a very natural amount of wrist break to use for the half-shot. The point that I'm trying to make in discussing the action of the hands on the backswing is that it becomes very, very difficult for you to hit any kind of golf shot if you are going to hit that shot totally stiff-wristed. In that instance, you become almost like a robot. And the message that your eye sends your brain and that your brain sends to the sensitive muscles in your hands and fingers is of no value anymore. Your tempo is destroyed because your hands and wrists are naturally a great part of the overall motion that determines tempo. It becomes very difficult for me to stand over a shot and say, "Well, how far back should I take my arms if I'm going to hold my hands and wrists totally rigid?" I don't think that very many people have the practice time, the energy or the determination to work out that kind of mechanical relationship. So I think it is far, far better to use your instincts. You'd be surprised to find just how much sensitivity and feel you do have in your fingertips, even if you are not a particularly good golfer. You'll never know until you can relax on a short shot and use more feel than mechanics.

Aside from allowing you to develop a more natural tempo, your natural sensitivity will help you to adjust to different conditions, when the greens are fast or slow, when the course is wet or when there is a stiff wind blowing. If you attempt to do everything mechanically then you are forced to practice every individual shot that could possibly arise on the golf course as conditions or circumstances change. When you allow your natural sense of feel to be the controlling factor of the shot, then you can simply program the varying elements of course condition and circumstance in your mind. Your eyes are a great help in programming your mind, so allow yourself to visualize your shots. And allow your mind to translate to your body in terms of feel. This makes your entire short game much easier to adapt to varying conditions.

One thing that I have not mentioned until now is the desired plane of the swing when hitting a short shot. When you are hitting a pitch shot it is very difficult to keep the face of the club pointing toward the hole if you are swinging on too flat a plane. When your hands move too quickly to the inside on the backswing and then into the ball from well inside of the line on the down stroke, there is a tendency for the hands to roll over to the left. This, again, will take the natural loft off the clubface, producing a low driving shot. So for short shots with the wedge, you have to take the club back more along the line that follows the target line; in other words, on a slightly more upright plane. But always keeping the hands in a similar position to the position for a full shot.

Your choice of club for a short shot is largely a matter of personal taste. Naturally, if you have a shot that you want to get way up in the air and stop quickly, you will go to the most lofted club in your bag, usually a sand iron. Don't be afraid to try pitching with your sand wedge. The really beautiful little shots that you admire on TV are usually executed with it. It can be used quite successfully as long as there is some kind of cushion under the ball. However, when you have a great deal of green to work with, stopping the ball quickly is not one of the most important facets of the shot. Then the choice of the club is a bit more a matter of debate. For a normal chip shot, where I want the ball to land just on the green and roll toward the hole, I use a 7-iron almost all the time. I think it's reasonable to go to a less lofted club if you have a tremendous amount of green between your ball and the hole, and you really need the ball to roll a long way. Conversely, you can use a more lofted club if you are right on the edge and faced with a shot of only ten to fifteen feet that cannot be properly stroked with a putter because of the lie. You might want to go to a 9-iron or even a wedge in this situation. I'm not certain as to exactly why I prefer the 7-iron for all of my normal chip shots, although it is a club that I have worked with quite a bit throughout the years. I feel very comfortable with a 7-iron in my hands. I think I'm much better off with this club than if I were to try and select a different club every time the length of the shot varied as little as ten or fifteen feet. I really think that, whatever club you feel more comfortable with, you should stay with it as much as possible on normal chip shots. That way you are not required to make a conscious decision as to which club you should use for every different little shot that you're confronted with. It's the same thing as with a full swing. You are naturally going to get much better at anything that you are able to repeat many, many times. So find a favorite club and then try and use it as often as you can.

Because I use the same club for most of my ordinary chip shots, there are certain variations in technique that come in as conditions change. Under normal circumstances I like to play all my chips and pitches from an address in which the ball is situated opposite my left heel. Bear in mind, though, that my feet are so close together that the inside of my left heel is close to the center of my stance. Now if the situation calls for me to hit a particularly hard driving shot that is a little lower than the shot I would normally hit, I simply move my hands forward a bit more at address, placing them in more of a leading position, taking some of the loft off the club. From this address position, if I make my normal swing, I will hit the ball a bit lower and it will run a bit harder. One thing that has worked very well for me in chipping is the idea of minimizing all motion on the backswing and the foreswing, reducing the stroke to its absolute essentials. I am always looking to make certain that the backswing I use is neither too long nor too short for the particular tempo that I am trying to achieve and the length of the shot that I want. When you allow your backstroke to get a bit too long, all of a sudden your subconscious mind comes in and says: Watch it, don't hit it too hard. What happens then is that you quit at the ball, either making imprecise contact or leaving the shot well short. Try to take only as long a backswing as you absolutely need. By doing this, you won't be afraid to accelerate crisply through the ball and, secondly, with a shortened stroke, the clubhead will tend to remain lower to the ground throughout the swing, producing more consistent contact. By keeping the clubhead low to the ground, just as in putting, you are more likely to produce a shot that will roll very well—and after all, the only reason that you use a less lofted club when chipping is to produce a shot that does roll, somewhat like a putt.

The actual stroke used in making a chip shot is just a miniature of the stroke that you use for a pitch shot, which in turn is simply a miniature of the full swing. Again, with the chip shot the wrists should be allowed to break naturally, although they will only break a very slight bit, due to the shortness of the stroke. The left hand is the leader coming into the ball and you should make every effort not to allow the right hand to come across the left at any time during the execution of this shot. The hands are placed gently on the club—not tight—to promote as much feel as possible. After just a little practice your two hands should begin to feel like one. Don't separate their actions to such a degree that they don't work together. I think it is very important to try to hit all of your normal chip shots with as little spin as possible. This means that you want to contact the ball squarely with the clubface looking down the intended line, the club moving down that line and the clubface moving more or less directly along the ground rather than down into the ball and through the ground. As soon as you begin hitting the ball from all sorts of varying angles, you put a great deal of spin on it and the shot will not react the same from time to time. It is much easier to control a shot without any great degree of spin than to try constantly to hit a hard spinning shot of one type or another. Every time you attempt to put spin on a golf shot you are adding another variable, and unless that spin is absolutely necessary in face of the conditions, you are complicating the whole game unnecessarily. In those instances when it is absolutely essential for you to put some sort of spin on the ball, it is important to remember that the mechanics of putting spin on a short shot are exactly the same as the mechanics of curving a long shot in flight. If you need a shot that gets up very quickly and stops abruptly upon landing, your only real choice is to cut the ball, striking it with an open clubface and a swing that is traveling from the outside to the inside of the target line. Before I went to see Bob Toski I had no real idea of how to cut the ball at all. This was one of the most important things that Bob taught me. And the method that he taught me is the simplest way that I can see of learning how to hit a cut shot. This applies to any shot that you are trying to put slicespin on, be it a short pitch or a full drive. Rather than making your normal swing along the target line, at the target, you should simply open up your stance somewhat and have the face of the club square to the intended target. Remember now that when you are going to cut the ball your intended line of swing is left of the flag or landing area in the fairway. Then, as you swing into the ball, if your swing line follows the line established by your address position, you will cut across the face of the ball with an open clubface, producing a shot that goes higher than normal and carries a great deal of spin. In hitting this shot with a wedge, one of the most difficult things for people to convince themselves to do is to allow the club to swing well to the left of the intended target. So many weekend players have a fear of pulling the ball that they instinctively push their hands toward the target at the last moment. And instead of producing a high cut shot, they will produce a low push shot that generally goes well to the right of the target and way past it. What you are trying to do when you cut the ball is to swing the club from the outside of the target line to the inside through the entire swing and to lead with the left side very strongly so that the clubface remains open with respect to the path of the swing. This is all rather easily accomplished with certain alterations in your address position and training your mind to allow the clubhead to swing across the intended line. In general, I try not to exaggerate any of these adjustments, although in certain circumstances it becomes necessary to try a shot with an extraordinary amount of spin on it. In this instance, I will lay my club way open and align myself way to the left of the target, much as I will in trying to cut a ball out of the sand trap. This, however, is a very dangerous shot, and I would not suggest that the casual player try it unless he or she has practiced it first. You are always better off playing the shot that does not demand perfection to get you on the green. Since most golfers mis-hit a great many shots to begin with, it is unreasonable to attempt a shot that has to be executed perfectly simply to get the ball on the green. You are far better off allowing yourself a margin for error, trying to hit a shot fifteen feet from the pin rather than two feet from the pin, if hitting it two feet from the pin requires that you cut the ball over the edge of a bunker and land it on only two or three feet of green.

Another shot that is very useful when you have to get the ball way up in the air, but your lie is heavy, preventing clean contact and a great deal of spin, is the soft, semi-explosion shot with either the sand or the pitching wedge. In this shot you must be aware that you are going to catch a few blades of grass between your clubface and the ball. And thus any chance of putting a great deal of spin on the ball will be eliminated, so instead of relying on spin to stop the shot, you are going to have to rely on great height and a soft landing. To make certain that you get the ball up quickly and softly, it is important to place your hands in a good leading position. Just as for an explosion from sand, the stance is open and the hands are ahead. The idea with this particular shot is to take a long, leisurely swing, leading the hands slowly and firmly *through* the grass and the ball. The key to getting the ball up in the air is a firm lead with the left side across the ball, from the outside to the inside of a line between the ball and the target.

As you would expect, the technique for hitting a low driving shot is exactly the opposite of the technique used in hitting a high floating shot. To hit those low punched-wedge shots that carry a great deal of spin, it is necessary to have the hands leading through impact, so that you can pinch the ball between the clubhead and the turf, driving it down and creating a maximum of backspin. As I read through most golf instructions and listen to amateurs speak about golf, I notice that there are a lot of fallacies concerning the action that is necessary to produce backspin on a short shot. For example, people are constantly talking of taking a huge divot when they are trying to put a lot of backspin on the ball. The fact is, you can put a great deal of backspin on any shot without taking so much as the slightest divot. Backspin is simply the result of the way the clubface hits the ball. The first and most important factor determining the degree of backspin that you get on a short shot is the precision with which the ball is struck. Most amateurs, without even knowing it, tend to hit about a quarter of an inch behind their wedge shots. And this quarter of an inch is sufficient to eliminate most of the backspin that would normally occur on a well-struck wedge. On a pitch shot, hitting a fraction behind the ball will generally not ruin the flight of the shot, but it will eliminate whatever chance you may have had of spinning the ball properly. What I'm getting at here is that an absolute must for achieving backspin is perfectly clean contact between the clubface and the golf ball. The only reason that you see good players taking a substantial divot when they are hoping to put a great deal of backspin on the ball is that it is much easier to avoid hitting the shot the slightest bit fat if the club is descending to the ball on a very steep angle. If the club is coming down into the ball from well above, there is very little chance that it will hit the ground prior to striking the ball. In addition, a steep angle of descent with the wedge forces the ball to ride up the face of the club, putting additional spin on it. A descending blow and clean contact make best use of the loft that is built into the club and also of the score lines across the face of the club, which are so important in playing short shots that the United States Golf Association actually sets limits in the Rules of Golf as to the width and depth allowed in these score lines. With this in mind, to hit a low spinning shot it is only logical to position the ball back toward your right foot, as this will make it less likely that you will contact the turf before striking the ball. In addition, positioning the ball back naturally places the hands ahead of the clubface, from which position a down-and-through striking action is encouraged.

One thing that you must remember in trying to hit the low spinning shot is that the left wrist must be kept very firm through impact so that the club may be held through the ball square to the target. This allows the ball to climb up the face and take on a great deal of spin. Firmness in the left wrist through impact is, to a great extent, a matter of strength and training. I think that is why you will see more good men golfers able to put a great deal of spin on the ball compared with most women. A lot of women players whom I see, feeling that they have insufficient strength in their wrists—especially the left wrist—are afraid to try to hold a good solid position of that wrist through impact, and thus they allow their hands to break down and the ball is struck imprecisely. Here again I'm returning to my familiar refrain about striking the ball solidly. This is something that I have found so important in every phase of the game that I just can't overstate it. I think if there is one thing a beginning golfer should concentrate on when trying to put together a good golf game, it would have to be striking the ball solidly.

The actual procedure used in deciding upon and then executing a short shot is usually a matter of logic and a knowledge of your own golf game. As I mentioned at the beginning of this chapter, the first thing you must do is check to see how much green you have to work with. Ideally you will have enough room with which to work so that you can hit a normal shot without trying to put any excessive height or spin on the ball, and can allow the ball to roll up naturally toward the hole. If circumstances demand that you put some sort of unnatural spin on the ball, you must think very carefully before deciding upon the particular shot. Always go with the shot that will leave you room to get away with a slight error rather than the shot that must be executed perfectly to get you on the green. Always make certain that you examine the lie prior to deciding upon the particular shot that you wish to use. Remember that it is almost impossible to put any amount of spin on the ball from a fluffy or spongy lie, particularly if the ball is in the rough. Your best bet in these circumstances is to try to stop the ball with a high soft shot rather than a spinning shot. If your lie is good and there is no apparent problem in making clean contact with the ball, try to select the shot that demands the least amount of spin to come off successfully. In other words, you should choose a straight forward pitch with a sand wedge rather than a high cut shot with a pitching wedge or a 9-iron. Always search for the simplest shot that will get the job done.

Once you have taken into account the length of the shot, the amount of green you have to work with, the lie of your ball, the condition of the fairway and the green and any weather conditions that may have a substantial influence on your shot, you should try to develop a mental picture of the desired shot, taking into account the trajectory, the landing area and the ball's flight to the pin. After you have made your decision as to the shot you wish to play, it is simply a matter of standing over the ball in a position that will encourage the striking action that you wish to produce.

Once you have adjusted your stance and alignment to suit the demands of the shot that you need, then it becomes very important, I feel, to allow your natural touch and sensitivity to take over. After you have set yourself up for a particular shot, simply retain in your mind a strong sense of your target and the trajectory that is needed to get the ball there. From this point on, it is fairly easy to allow your natural feeling to take over and, if you are able to do this, chances are that the shot will be successful.

SAND PLAY

For a normal bunker shot, a blast-type shot, I would address the ball very much the same as I do a pitch shot: keep the ball fairly far forward inside my left heel—right on the left heel. I find I get into the most trouble when I don't position the ball correctly. It's important that the ball is positioned properly and my stance is fairly open. I'm trying to get the feeling that I can swing slightly from the outside with the face of the blade square to the target. Hitting the sand shot is very much the same thing as trying to cut the ball. It depends on the swing of the club on the outside to the inside and your effort to cut the ball out of the sand. In this particular shot I do break my wrists a little sooner; there is an actual effort to break a little sooner. One reason is that it helps to put more action in the hands. It helps to cut the ball out of the sand and it's an important fact that in swinging the club slightly across the line I am trying to lead with my left hand and left side. There is not a great deal of movement in my body in general or in the lower part of my body but I don't totally restrict it either. I just let that go and do whatever comes naturally. But it's basically a hand-and-arm shot. What I'm trying to say is that I am causing the face of the blade to go through to the hole while I'm trying to swing the club across the line; I am trying to keep that club from turning over. At address, the blade is set open and I'm trying to pull the club across the ball and keep the blade square to the target line, not the swing line. With respect to the swing line, the blade is actually open. Because I'm trying to get the club a little bit to the outside on sand shots, I use the wrist break to help me get it there. A quick break in the wrists is very useful. It helps me to get the club at least on the line or outside of the target line, and not inside the line. If it gets inside the line, it makes it difficult to cut the ball out of the sand.

I learned to play sand shots by picking the spot behind the ball and trying to make the club hit that spot in the sand and cut beneath the ball. The position of the spot varies, depending on how far you need to hit the ball. The further you want the ball to go, the closer to the ball that spot would be, because you want to take less sand. I don't really use the spot method any more. I've gotten so used to playing these shots that it's more a matter of instinct with me. The amount of sand that you take beneath the ball is another very important factor. I think one significant aspect of sand play that people forget is the question of how deep a cut to make under the ball. Too many people think that hitting behind the ball means digging the

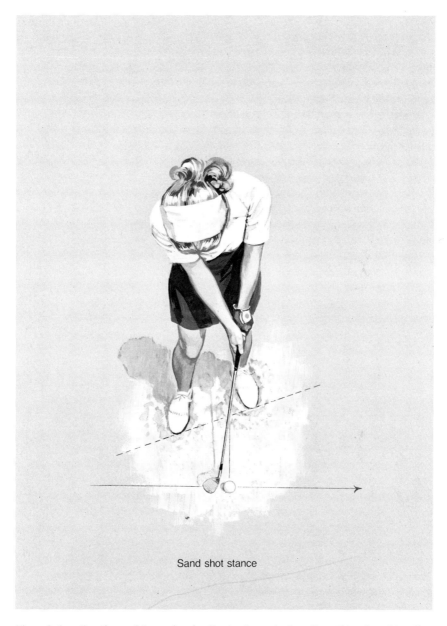

Sand shot stance

The relative directions of the swing for the basic explosion. Everything is set to allow you to swing across the target line from the outside, cutting the ball from the sand with an open clubface. Because the clubface is open with respect to the stance and direction of the swing, the ball will not be thrown in the direction of the swing, but rather to the right of the swing line, toward the target.

Sand shots

The explosion shot. By opening your stance, you are able to swing the club across the ball from the outside, slicing beneath it and tossing it softly to the green. Picture a saucer of sand beneath the ball that you're trying to cut from the trap and throw onto the green.

clubhead straight down into the sand like a pickax. The clubhead should actually pass through the sand in a shallow arc, cutting a thin slice of sand from under the ball. That will give you a bit more feel for the distance required and will also allow you to put some spin on the ball. If you dig too deeply into the sand, you will have to take an awfully hard swing to hit the required shots. If you can get the feel of leading the clubface through with the left hand while holding it square to the hole, the explosion shot should present no special problems.

10

Putting

To assume my putting grip, I place my left hand on the putter with the thumb straight up and down the shaft. This is a different grip than the one that I normally use for my full shot, and understandably so, because the sole requisites for good putting are accuracy and a delicate touch. Power is of no value on the green, and thus the power to be had from my normal grip can be sacrificed for the sake of accuracy. When the back of the left hand faces the target, the hand is not liable to flex or cock during the stroke. A weak grip with the left hand limits motion in the hands, and this is desirable on the green.

The right hand is placed on the shaft with the thumb straight down and the palm facing directly toward the hole. This weak position discourages motion and promotes a simple, well-controlled stroke. The index finger of my left hand overlaps the last two fingers of my right hand. I think that it is very important to get the entire right hand comfortably on the club, because a right-handed player naturally has more feeling in the right hand, and this should be taken advantage of. The putter sits at the roots of the fingers in the right hand, and you should feel as though you are cradling the club very gently with the entire right hand. I try to hold the club with a modified pistol grip in the right index finger, with the grip resting more toward the fingertip and the entire finger drawn up somewhat, allowing me to pinch the putter very lightly between my thumb and index finger. This gives me a better sense of control in the right hand. The important thing to remember is that the grip with the putter must be very, very light. I would guess that ninety-nine out of every hundred amateurs hold the putter too firmly. This deadens your natural sense of touch and prevents your making a smooth stroke.

Try taking a normal putting grip with an ordinary pencil, holding with just enough pressure to prevent its falling from your hands. That will be all the pressure needed to control your putter during the stroke.

In the address posture used for putting, the hands should be dead even with the ball or slightly ahead. The shaft should run straight up and down or be inclined a bit toward the hole. It must never lean back, and the hands should never get behind the ball. If the hands are behind, the wrists are automatically broken from the outset, and it is very likely that you will get too loose with the stroke. When the wrists get "flippy" it is too easy to get the clubhead moving ahead of your stroke, and you will be forced to help the putter head along rather than allowing it to swing freely. So it's a matter of personal taste whether you choose to have your hands even with or slightly ahead of the ball, as long as you don't allow them to drift behind the ball. My arms are fairly close to my body because I feel more stable that way and I think I can repeat the position more often.

I like to stand over the ball with most of my weight on my left foot. This discourages any motion in my legs, trunk, or head. I don't like to think consciously in terms of no movement at all, because this can force you to freeze over the putt and become too tense. If you simply place most of your body weight solidly on the left foot and keep it set there throughout your stroke, there is little likelihood of a damaging body movement. It is important to find a balance between the rigid, mechanical position that destroys any natural fluidity and the loose, sloppy posture that encourages a great deal of wasted motion.

When I set up, I like to have the feeling that my eyes are directly over the ball. It seems to me that it's easier to retain a sense of the line from the ball to the target if your eyes are directly over the ball; moreover, I'd say that all very good putters have their eyes directly over the ball. It's simply a good perspective from which to judge the line.

The exact procedure that I use to assume my putting stance is the same from putt to putt. I more or less attack the ball from behind, standing slightly behind it so that I can see the line to the hole clearly. Then I am very careful about setting my putterhead down exactly perpendicular to the intended line of the putt. I don't set the putter down casually, as many amateurs will. I try to aim at a very specific point—either the exact center of the hole, one of the edges, or a spot to one side or the other if the slope of the green demands.

After I've set the putter, I am very careful not to disturb its exact alignment. Putting is a very precise affair, and the set of the blade at address is the most important factor in determining the alignment of your whole body. I attempt to set my feet and my body parallel to the line down which I intend

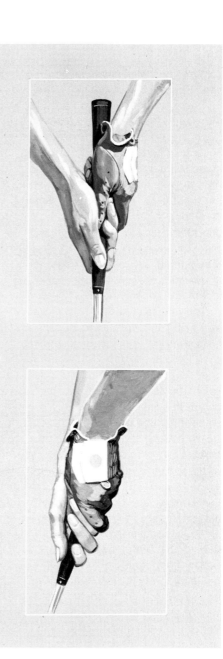

Putting grip

The completed putting grip. The club is held gently in the fingers of the right hand, with the left index finger overlapping the last two fingers of the right hand. Both thumbs are placed straight down the center of the shaft, with the left hand in a "weak" position, as power is unnecessary.

to move the putterhead. When my stance is complete, I want everything to be at a right angle to the target line.

Once I'm set over the ball, I try to look from the hole back to my ball and vice versa, in order to allow my eyes to help my sense of touch along. There is no particular number of looks that I like to take, but usually I will look up at least two or three times to make certain that I have a strong image in my mind's eye of the exact distance required. The messages sent through your eyes to your brain really have quite a bit to do with the touch and feel for distance that you acquire. It's very similar to the feel you have for driving a car. Be careful, though, not to stand over the ball for such a long time that you freeze. You must take the time to develop a proper mix of deliberation and relaxation. You should always feel comfortable just prior to beginning your actual stroke.

My main concerns in stroking the ball are keeping the putterhead low and square to the intended line and producing very solid contact.

The left hand is the dominant hand in determining the exact path of the stroke, but the right hand provides most of the touch, since the right hand is usually the most sensitive hand for the right-handed golfer. Actually, when I putt well, I don't have the sensation of two individual hands—it feels more as though they are one on the club. The left hand swings the putter away from the ball and, as the head of the putter begins swinging back toward the hole, the right hand regulates the exact striking force. The back of the left hand should never break down through or past impact, even as the right hand applies force. You should feel that the back of the left hand is moving toward the target even after the ball is on its way. At the very end of the stroke, particularly on longer putts, the left hand will break naturally, and this need not be consciously resisted.

I always try to keep the putterhead square to the line during the entire stroke. To me this is a natural part of the putting stroke. I make certain very slight, instinctive movements with my hands and arms in order to keep the face of the putter square; there is no forced rotation of my hands. The reason I am able to keep the putter square to the line with no forced manipulation is the combination arm-and-wrist stroke that I use. By employing my arms and hands to make the stroke, I am able to distribute any rotation over the full length of my arms, and thus the rotation at any one point in my hands or arms will be very slight. As a basic putting method, I don't believe in turning the putter or the wrist into an open position going back and then closing everything during the forward stroke. I realize that this "swinging-gate" style works very well for some people, but I think that it introduces one more possible source of error. Any time you can eliminate a potential trouble spot, you have got to be better off.

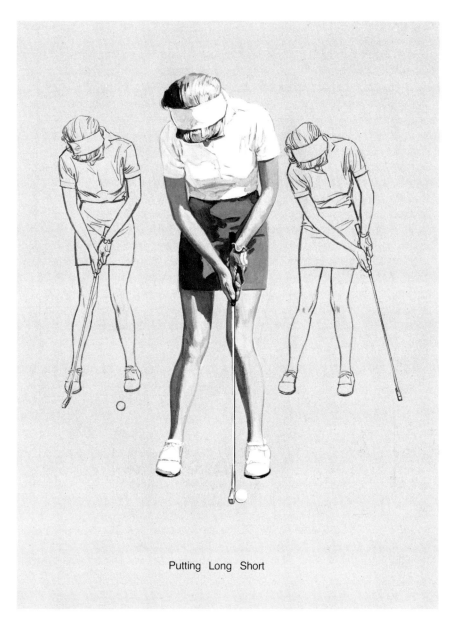

Putting Long Short

For any putt, long or short, make an even, well-paced and balanced stroke. The backstroke should be long enough to allow you to accelerate the putter very gradually to the ball, but not so long as to force you to slow down the stroke as you approach impact. The followthrough should be the natural result of the stroke, its length dictated by the length of your backstroke.

To set the putter in motion, I don't use a forward press, although many good putters find it important as an aid in getting the hands started. Once I get the putter blade lined up in a perfect position, I don't want to disturb the alignment in any way, shape, or form. I like the feeling of beginning my stroke from an exact position so that I have a clear picture of the desired set of the blade throughout the stroke. With a forward press, the blade of the putter has to move slightly, and my sense of squareness is disturbed.

A very important aspect of the stroke that is mentioned in almost every bit of golf instruction is disregarded by nearly every amateur golfer that I see. I am speaking of keeping the head of the putter low to the ground during the backstroke and through impact. And it is a very easy thing to discipline yourself to do. Keeping the blade low improves your chances for a solid hit, and a solid hit is critical in producing a well-rolling putt. I used to work very hard on keeping the blade low well into the followthrough, but I have decided that there is no need to force the putterhead along the ground through the finish of the stroke. If you can keep it low going back and low just past impact, it is all right to allow the clubhead to rise naturally at the end of the stroke. So long as you keep it low going through the ball, you should be guaranteed solid contact. And I think that you would be surprised to see how many putts are missed because they are not struck solidly. Any golfer can line up the blade fairly accurately, and from that point on solid contact is the most important factor. I see many weekend golfers with good strokes missing too many putts. Whether they are aware of it or not, most of these missed putts are the result of imprecise contact— the center of the putter face fails to meet the back of the ball and the putt is immediately off the intended line. A low stroke and the thought of solid striking will help a good number of golfers on the greens.

A common problem among these players who are considered poor putters is the judgment of distance on long putts. Lack of touch on the longer ones is almost a sure source of three-putt greens, and nothing can be more aggravating than a long string of three-putts in the midst of a good tee-to-green round. In all putts, as far as gauging distance is concerned, the length of the backstroke is the controlling factor. For a long putt I'm naturally going to make a longer backstroke than for a short putt. By varying the length of my stroke, I can maintain a constant tempo from stroke to stroke. I am not forced to speed up my action to hit the ball harder.

For a long putt, I want to take a long enough backstroke to allow me to lead my hands and the putterhead out toward the target after the ball has been hit. I don't want to make so long a backstroke that I subconsciously feel a need to slow down the putterhead as I approach impact. I am trying for a stroke that can be smooth and rhythmic, allowing me to make a natural followthrough. At one time I worked on the theory that the followthrough should be twice as long as the backstroke. I think that that's a good thought to keep in mind when practicing; it gets the head of the putter and your hands moving out toward the hole and prevents the stabbing stroke that really ruins you on the green. The idea of moving the hands along the line well into the followthrough is very important if you are to develop a consistent stroke. If your hands stop at the ball, or if you allow your left hand to break at the moment contact is made, it is an indication that you have begun to slow down the stroke prior to impact. Allowing the stroke to decelerate as you approach the ball destroys the natural swinging action of the putter, and it becomes difficult to keep the stroke constant.

It almost goes without saying that the most critical part of good approach is solid striking. The entire concept of feel is based upon your ability to strike the back of the ball with the sweet spot (dead center) of the putter nearly every time you step up to a putt. If you strike the ball with different parts of the putter from putt to putt, you will always have a hard time developing a sense of touch. You will never feel the same thing twice, and the ball will never react the same way coming off the face of the putter.

One important aspect of putting that I have not mentioned until now is the problem of reading greens and determining the exact line upon which the ball will travel to the hole. I usually try to read the green from behind the ball, so that I am able to develop an image of the exact route that the putt will travel. I rarely walk around to the other side of the hole and look back at the ball, because then the picture of my line is reversed. Some people find it very useful to view the line from both sides, and I can understand this, particularly on downhill putts where you can look back up into the hill and possibly can see something that was not apparent from above the hole.

One of the aids that I have used over the years to read greens is plumb-bobbing. Plumb-bobbing is standing behind the ball, facing the hole, and holding your putter so that it hangs straight down in front of your master eye. The head of the putter should obscure your view of your ball. If you hang the putter in this fashion and then look up at the flag stick, you will notice that on a sloping green, the flag stick appears on one side of the hanging club, if the clubhead is kept on a direct line with the ball. The side of the putter shaft on which the flag stick appears is the high side of the hole. I find plumb-bobbing to be of the most value in reading a putt that you know will break but can't quite figure out in which direction. I don't use it to determine the exact line of my putt, however. If, for instance, the putter shaft appears to fall half an inch to the left of the hole, I know that the putt will break to my right, but I won't use the half-inch as an exact guideline.

There are many putts which, because of the terrain, can be real foolers; you can't really tell which way the ball will break simply by looking at them. In these cases, plumb-bobbing is a great help.

Grain is a factor that I consider very carefully when I'm reading a green. In certain places, grain does not influence the roll of the putt as strongly as in others. Bent grasses, as a general rule, are less grainy than Bermuda grasses. In a climate that demands the use of Bermuda grass, you are likely to encounter a great deal of grain. In Florida, for instance, it is impossible to putt well without a knowledge of reading grain. On Bermuda greens, you will only rarely be able to see the grain simply by looking at the blades of grass. On bent greens, it is possible actually to see which way the blades are lying, so reading the grain is no big problem. With Bermuda, you have to find a few little tricks to help you in finding the grain. As a basic rule with Bermuda, keep in mind that it tends to grow towards the setting sun. So you will generally find that the grain runs from east to west. In Florida, I've found this to be true most of the time.

As an aid in checking my first impression of the grain, it is often possible simply to look at the cup. If the hole has been in one spot for a long time, you'll find that the grass on one edge of the cup will have turned brown and died. The side of the hole with the brown grass is usually the side toward which the grain is running, because the roots of the grass have been cut away on the side of the cup, while only the tips of the blades have been cut on the side that is still green. So you can get a good picture of which way the grass is growing.

The grain on a Bermuda green can also be seen by checking the actual appearance of the grass from one side of the green to the other. If you walk around a green and look at the grass from all sides, you will notice that the green appears to shine from one viewpoint and appears dull when viewed from the opposite side. Whenever you see a shine on the green, you are looking with the grain. This is usually what professionals are looking for when they walk around an entire green while lining up a putt.

If you find yourself playing on bent greens that are particularly grainy and difficult to read, it is safe to assume that the grass is growing in the direction of the drainage, toward the low side of the green. Because of this, the grain is most likely to be growing with the slopes of the green, so it is rare to have a putt that does not break with the slope. On most bent-grass greens, there is no real need to worry about the effect of grain.

As long as we are on the subject of grain and grasses, let me bring up another area of the game that is really affected by the terrain on and around the greens—chipping and pitching. Grain is a very big consideration when you are hitting any sort of short shot. If you are chipping into the grain, it is

Putting—reading greens

When you are faced with a breaking putt, it is important that you pay particular attention to the line on which you want the putt to start. Align yourself parallel to this original line, then stroke the ball firmly down that line as though you were playing a straight putt to an imaginary hole on one side or the other of the actual hole.

very important that you make clean contact, because the grass will prevent your getting away with a shot that's even slightly fat. Naturally, a chip-shot hit into the grain will stop quicker, and a chip that is hit into the fringe when the grain is against you is liable to stop dead in its tracks as the longer grass catches it.

When you are chipping or pitching with the grain, it is a bit easier to play the fancy shots because, with the grass lying in the direction of your stroke, you can slide the clubhead over the ground with no fear of having the grass grab it and ruin the shot.

In all cases, whether you are chipping or putting, remember that the variables influencing your shot—grain, slope, distance and ground conditions—are all factors that must be programmed in your mind before you are set to make the actual stroke. Once you have settled on a shot for the situation, it is important to clear your mind of all technical thoughts. Simply concentrating on solid contact is enough to occupy your mind during any shot. When you are trying to decide upon the exact stroke that is right for the situation, it is a good idea to visualize the shot coming off successfully. This is particularly true on the greens, as putting is the most precise area of the game and, because you are dealing with no great distances, the easiest shots to visualize. I can picture the path of a putt as it goes into the hole, and this is a good positive image to have as you stand over a putt. If you can form a clear visual picture of something that you want to accomplish, it's more likely that you will succeed. I never step up to a shot without having some visual picture of what I want that shot to do. I play very poorly when I just stand up and hit away with no mental preparation. I think that proper visualization is the key to a positive attitude on the green. You hear so often that putting is seventy-five per cent mental, and most of that seventy-five per cent depends upon your ability to maintain a clear picture once you are set to make your stroke. Many times when I am lining up a putt, I can actually see a path over the green that will get the ball in the hole. I like the feeling of trying to stroke the ball along that imaginary line. I am not a player who likes to putt over a particular spot between my ball and the hole. As with the rest of my game, once I have sifted through all of the information that applies to my shot, I let my instincts take over. When you have trained yourself not to interfere with your inborn sense of feel, all of your so-called touch shots, especially your putts, will naturally become less difficult.

11

Playing the
Terrain

When playing from an unusual lie of any sort, the first thing that I keep in mind is balance. Standing on a hill tends to disrupt your balance during the golf swing. And if you will think of minimizing your movement, the chances of your hitting a good shot off an unusual lie will be greatly improved. Any time the terrain disrupts your stance, you should first look at the manner in which the slope of ground on which you are forced to stand will affect your golf swing. Try to realize what parts of your swing the stance will tend to exaggerate. Then try to compensate for these exaggerations in your address position. For example, when the ball is lying above the level of your feet in a side-hill lie, the most important thing that you should do is get a little bit further away from it, to give yourself more room to swing. When the ball is higher than usual in relation to your body, it will be closer to your hands, and thus you will not have as much room in which to work the club as you make the shot. So the simple, logical thing to do in this circumstance is to stand a little further away from the ball and choke up on the club a bit. By choking up on the club you make it much easier for yourself to hit the ball first and not the ground.

The idea with unusual lies is always to try to swing the club along the lines of the terrain. On a side-hill lie with the ball a bit above your feet it is important to remember to aim the ball somewhat to the right of the target, because from this lie the clubface will be tilted in such a way that the loft built into the clubface will send the ball not only up into the air but also off toward the left. In addition, when the ball is higher than normal in relation to your body, the swing will tend to flatten, causing you to come into the ball from well inside the target line and your hands to turn over much more quickly than usual.

Simple common sense would indicate that, when you find yourself facing a shot with the ball below your feet, you have to figure out a way to get closer to the ball, because just by the nature of the lie the ball is further away from your hands than normal. When most amateurs attempt to play this shot, they begin from a starting position which would be all right for a flat lie but which in no way takes into account the special problems that arise when the ball is sitting below their feet. Somewhere in the course of their swing the subconscious mind takes over, reminding them that they're not going to get to the ball as readily as if it were on a flat lie, so they lunge at the ball, attempting to lengthen their swing—and the result is usually a topped shot or a fat shot. If you get down close enough to the ball in your starting position, make yourself comfortable, then you can make a normal swing and hit a good shot. The key in hitting this shot is to be certain that you get the clubface down flush with the ball. To do this it is necessary that you bend more from the waist at address and retain that angle of tilt throughout your swing, making certain that your head is not raised or lowered at any point. Get close enough so that you will not have to go to your toes to reach the ball. Since you're bending over more from the very beginning, you are automatically adjusting the path of your swing to suit the roll of the terrain. When you make this shot, be sure that you aim off a bit to the left, allowing for a slight fade, since the greater degree of bend in your waist will encourage a more upright swing and less rotation of the hands into the impact area. If you still find yourself having problems making solid contact after these adjustments in your address posture, you might try hitting it a bit more off your back foot, as this will encourage you to get to the ball a bit quicker with your swing.

For an uphill lie, where the tilt of the hill forces you to lean somewhat away from the target, it is important to remember that most of your weight will be thrown toward your right side and that this will make it difficult to maintain your balance throughout the swing. Rather than attempting to fight the terrain, allow your body to work with it. The slope of the ground will force your right side to be distinctly lower than it would be for a normal shot. This is fine if you accept the fact that there will be some swing changes that occur naturally because of this setup. Since all of your weight is being pushed toward your right or downhill foot, it is important to avoid making too big a transfer of weight during the backswing, as it will be very difficult for you to shift to your left coming into the ball. You will then be forced to shift your weight uphill. One thing which really helps me is to stay very solidly on my left side during the swing, eliminating the large transfer of weight to the right leg that I use on most normal swings. With the weight kept on the left side throughout the shot, it is very easy to contact the ball without falling back on your right side. Since you are going uphill, it is no real problem to achieve sufficient height on the shot.

For an uphill lie, I like to play the ball more toward my forward foot, because the slope of the terrain tends to tilt my body in such a fashion that the hitting area—the small flat area in which solid contact may be made—is moved forward into the hill. If you stand on a severe uphill lie and swing for a few moments, you will notice immediately that your swing does not tend to level off to meet the terrain until the clubhead is almost up to your left toe. Consequently, I find that this is the most desirable ball position for that shot. With a severe uphill lie you may want to consider taking a less lofted club than the distance would demand and hitting the shot with almost a half-swing, so that the ball does not go too high up in the air. If you are using extremely lofted clubs from a sharp uphill lie, chances are that you'll hit the ball so high that you lose a lot of your distance. In addition, it is a good idea when you are hitting this shot to aim off a few yards to the right, since the land will force you to stay behind the ball much better than you normally would, promoting a shot that draws slightly from the right to the left.

The severe downhill lie, where the golfer is leaning toward his or her target, presents the most problems for a majority of amateur players. The most important swing adjustment to be made is to move the ball back slightly in your stance, more toward your uphill foot. This will allow you to strike the ball before striking the hill, which is the major problem in playing a steep downhill shot. It may also be of some help to choke up on the club a little bit, as this will encourage your striking the ball cleanly before the club touches the turf. The biggest problem with the downhill lie is that the hill is, in essence, in the way of the back of the ball, so you have to strike down more abruptly to contact the ball cleanly. In playing from this sort of lie, it is more important to recognize that your body will be tilted more toward the target than is usual and that your right shoulder and the right side of your body will be higher than they would be for a normal fairway shot. You should attempt to align your shoulders so that they parallel the slope of the hill, rather than trying to assume a normal stance with the right shoulder lower than the left. If you do the latter, you will be fighting the slope of the land and making the shot much more difficult than it need be. If you're faced with a really severe downhill lie, I find that it helps to swing the club on a more upright plane, with the hands moving toward the ball more from above than from behind. With a more upright swing, the clubhead is descending more abruptly and so it is more likely that it will get to the ball cleanly without contacting the hill first. Keep in mind that these adjustments—the ball positioned more toward the right foot, swinging in a more upright plane—will tend to produce a shot that curves from left to right in flight, since your weight will be forced onto your left side more quickly and your hands will not be approaching the ball from inside the line as is normal. Naturally the path of your swing, when faced with a severe downhill lie, will tend to produce a shot that goes much lower than you would expect from a flat fairway lie. Consequently you should use a more lofted club and plan on producing a driving shot as opposed to the high soft shot that you would hit from the flat or slightly uphill lie. The fundamental approach to keep in mind when playing from an unusually hilly lie is as follows: Always try to swing and keep good balance if the lie is such that it will force you to make an exaggerated shift in weight to one side of the body or the other. You should concentrate on making the swing that involves the least amount of weight transference as is possible to achieve the required distance, even if it means going to a much longer club than you would normally use. The key to successful shots from hilly lies is aligning your body so that you are tilted in accordance with the slope of the ground. This means that from a severe uphill lie, you should not be trying to maintain a stance in which your right shoulder is slightly below your left. Rather, you should accept the fact that your body is rotated toward the right, and stand up to the ball with the right side of your body way below the left. By positioning your body so that you follow the slope of the ground, you will be more likely to swing the clubhead along the terrain and produce solid contact. Be aware, though, that shifts in your address position will force some changes in the character of your swing, which in turn will affect the shape of your shot. So while you adjust your stance, make certain that you adjust your aim to compensate for the change in your swing pattern. If these changes are made sensibly, and if you are willing to accept the fact that unusual adjustments are necessary for unusual lies, you will be able to swing with the hill, rather than fighting it, and your shotmaking will become much more consistent as a result.

IV
Bringing Your Mind to Bear

12

Shotmaking and
Maneuvering the Ball

When discussing alignment, I made use of the terms "swing line," "target line," and "clubface alignment," and suggested that these variables control the direction and shape of any individual golf shot. It is possible to describe any golf shot that curves using these three terms. For a right-handed golfer, a hook will occur any time the clubface is pointing to the left of the swing line through impact. Any time the clubface is in this closed position, the shot will tend to curve from right to left in flight. The ultimate destination of your shot with respect to the intended target is determined by the relationship of the swing line to the target line at the moment of impact. If the swing line is moving across the target line from left to right, which is inside to outside from the golfer's perspective, the shot will tend to start to the right of the target and then hook back toward the flag. Of course, if your clubface is closed with respect to the swing line and that swing line is pointing way left of the target to begin with, then you will make a pulled hook or a left-to-left shot, which is generally ruinous.

Similarly, if the clubface is open or pointing more to the right than the swing line at the moment of impact, you will come up with a shot that curves from left to right in flight, either a fade or the more severe slice. This is by far the most common shot pattern for the average golfer. If the swing line is crossing the target line from outside to inside at the moment of impact and the clubface is open with respect to that swing line, the result will be a pulled slice, an awful-looking shot that begins left of the original target, then swings back toward the right side of the target in a large, rainbow-like arc. This is one of the weakest of all possible golf shots.

If, at the moment of impact, the clubface is open with respect to the swing line and the swing line is moving to the right of the intended target from the inside to the outside, then the result will be a pushed slice, a shot that's as ugly and every bit as painful as a pulled hook.

These double-cross shots—in which both the clubhead and the swing line are crossing lines in the same direction, producing a shot that goes from bad to worse—are shots that must be eliminated if you intend to bring your golf scores down significantly.

One of the real troubles with allowing for a big hook or slice in your golf game is that you get to hitting across lines that way; in my idea of playing the game, it doesn't work very well since your alignment pattern becomes confused and it's therefore difficult to have a proper projection of target in your mind. I've programmed myself to hit the ball and swing the club along particular lines right out toward the target. As a result, I don't feel as though I'm able to play for a large curve and still retain my normal swing pattern.

If I'm inclined to cross the target line to any degree, I'm more apt to do it in an attempt to draw the ball, because this involves crossing the target line slightly from inside to out, which to my mind is not a bad swing pattern. So I feel more comfortable trying to swing slightly away from myself—trying to hit a hook—than I do when I want to hit it left-to-right, the reason being that when I want to cut the ball or fade it, there is a tendency for me to exaggerate the outside-in action. Rather than a gentle fade, I wind up with a left-to-right shot that is not controlled well enough!

Fading the ball off the tee, generally speaking, is a very slight movement. There are very few instances in which you are actually trying to hit a banana ball. But for some reason I always seem to overexaggerate a fade. So rather than worry myself with crossing lines and swinging from outside the target line to inside the target line, I find that it is easier for me to stand on the tee and try to hit my normal shot, perhaps driving my left hand a little more strongly through the impact area, holding the clubface open and producing a gentle fade. In maneuvering the ball, exaggerations are the very thing that I am hoping to avoid. Every time that I speak of moving a shot from left to right or from right to left, I am speaking of a gentle draw or a gentle fade. There are very, very few instances in which you would want the golf ball to curve a great deal in flight. So everything that I do as far as my shotmaking goes is geared to eliminating the exaggerations and making certain that all movements of the golf ball in flight are gentle ones. It is for this reason that I don't feel comfortable teeing up my ball on the extreme right or left of a tee, because that seems to encourage a harshly curved shot. It just doesn't work very well for me.

The only time I will move to one extreme corner of the tee is when moving will give me a much wider angle of approach into the fairway. There are times when, by getting on one side of the tee or the other, you can actually give yourself more room to drive to; you see more room from that perspective, and this allows you to hit the shot with a bit more confidence. That is terribly important.

As long as I've played golf, my natural shot pattern has been from right to left, the pattern that I am the most familiar with. And if I just stand up and swing at the ball in the most natural fashion, I find that the result is a shot with a slight bit of draw on it. I've never really tried to get rid of this draw; in fact, I prefer it to hitting a straight ball because it seems to give me a good deal more distance. What I don't like to do, in general, is hook the ball. A soft draw is fine, but a big roundhouse hook is something that I very rarely seek. There are times when I might try to hit a shot that moves more from right to left than the normal draw, on holes that are wide open where I can just let everything go and roll the ball out there as far as possible. In this case, you are almost cheating a bit, using a big hook, to get a few extra yards in a situation where distance is your only concern. But that is really the only time when I like to see a big hook, other than trouble shots where you must necessarily go to certain extremes.

I think that a player's shotmaking ability—his or her ability to control the shape of each shot—can have a tremendous effect on the degree of distance that the individual is able to attain. Although my natural shot pattern is from right to left to draw the ball, I have now gotten a certain feel with my swing such that I can make the ball move slightly from left to right in a gentle fade, and I find that this shot is most important in the left-to-right cross wind. A player who can use a little bit of added distance must learn to use the wind to best advantage and never to fight it. You've got to learn off the tee how to make the ball ride the wind even though the wind isn't at your back, to get the ball moving in a pattern that will allow the wind to be at its back, in a manner of speaking.

It may be a very nice, accurate way to play—to hit the ball against a cross wind, holding it to a straight flight simply by employing spin—but this type of play costs you too much yardage. For myself and most of the players that I speak with and watch, that loss of yardage is too high a cost. So rather than fighting the wind, you can actually take advantage of it, making a windy day work on your side to give you a little bit of extra distance. With a right-to-left wind confronting me off a tee, I will set up to hit a shot that also moves from right to left, thus allowing the ball to move, for the most part, with the flow of the wind. In order to hit a shot that moves from right to left, you must set up in a position that will encourage the clubface to be slightly closed with respect to the swing line as you strike the ball. Remember now, every time that I speak of a shot that curves in flight, I am speaking of a shot that starts to one side of the target and then works back toward the target. No shot that curves in flight can be aimed directly at the target, since then it will be working away from the desired destination from the moment it leaves the clubface. Thus every time I speak of hitting a draw, keep in mind that I want the shot to start to the right of the target.

To encourage a shot that begins to the right of the target, I address the ball in a position that sets me up to swing the clubhead on a line to the right of my target line. In simpler terms, I just close my stance. With my stance closed, my clubhead will tend to swing along the line to the right of the target through impact, and the clubface will be closing a little sooner because the club is swinging more from the inside to the outside with the closed stance; and with the clubface looking at the target through impact, the desired relationship of a clubface that is closed to the swing line will be established. Thus the shot will draw in flight.

With the swing that I am teaching in this book, the full release and long extension of the hands and clubhead out and away from the body encourage a shot that moves from right to left. Therefore the player, upon learning my method, should have little if any trouble hitting a draw.

When I introduced the idea of using your shotmaking to increase your effective length on the golf course, I mentioned that I found a faded shot to be of great help when playing with a left-to-right cross wind. I had gone through a spell, trying to play the fade, when I either would not fade at all or would fade too much. I was getting into a pattern of exaggeration, a pattern that I disliked very much. To hit a cut shot—a shot that works from left to right in flight—all you have to do is make the opposite adjustments to those you make when attempting to hit a draw. You should line up in a position that will encourage you to swing the clubhead on a line to the left of the target. Keep the clubface in a position square to the target and swing the club from the outside to the inside, which forces the hands to release later, prompted by a pulling action with the left hand to produce a slightly open clubface. You will fashion a shot that begins from the left of the intended target and swings back toward it in flight.

In addition to controlling the direction that a shot will take in flight, it is very important for the golfer to be able to determine the height at which he or she wants the ball to travel. Obviously, on a windy day, high or low shots can provide an extraordinary advantage when it comes to achieving maximum distance. But more than this, an ability to control the height of each particular shot will allow you to take maximum advantage of the conditions that you find from course to course. For instance, the lush fairways of the Northeast tend to afford the player very little roll, so it becomes im-

Intentional hook—slice

To play an intentional draw or fade, you must align your body and feet to allow you to swing the clubhead across the target line from one side or the other—the target being where you intend to start the ball. In both instances, the clubface will be square to the target at impact, but will be moving across the target line, producing a shot that curves in flight.

portant to drive the ball a good distance through the air, not relying on much forward movement once it's touched down. For the player who is unable to hit high tee shots, in this instance, the game becomes a very difficult one. Conversely, on the hard fairways of Texas, the player who can hit a low running shot has quite an advantage over the player who can hit only high shots, and thus cannot make the best of the conditions.

The mechanics of controlling the height of your golf shots are actually fairly simple. The first thing that I would do to hit a high shot would be to play the ball a bit more forward in my stance than normal. In other words, if I normally have the ball about opposite my left heel, I might move it up to a point opposite my left toe. This will allow me to catch the ball just a little bit on the upswing, with my hands behind, rather than even with the club-face. This tends to increase the effective loft of the club, as compared to a normal shot. I move the ball in my stance so that I can take it on the upswing without any feeling of consciously lifting the ball. The clubhead simply catches the ball at a later point in the swing. And at this point it's already moving in an upward path.

There are times when, if I really want to hit the ball high and get it up quickly, I feel that I have to move the club in more of an upright plane. What this does is to cut down that flat area at the bottom of the swing, thus allowing the club to move in more of an up-and-down path through impact.

Because you have eliminated some of that all-important flat area at the bottom of the swing, you must make a conscious effort to hit the ball absolutely flush. It becomes imperative to stay down on the ball and not be in such a hurry to see whether it went up over that tree or not. If you do allow your upper body to pop up prematurely, you are going to hit high on the ball and, instead of hitting a shot way up in the air, you will probably hit one that barely gets off the ground. What you really need to do to hit the ball high is to get the clubhead low on the ball at impact. If you can get the force of the hit acting on the underside of the ball, the shot will tend to fly much higher. In some severe instances it can be to your advantage to attempt to fade the ball a little bit to get it up more quickly, using the same methods outlined for a fade that we've talked of before. An open clubface combined with a ball position that is a little further forward in your stance will produce about as high a shot as possible.

To hit the ball low it is absolutely essential that you have the feeling of leading the clubface with your hands and striking firmly down and through the shot, almost as though you were trying to drive the ball into the ground. But this feeling is more one of pushing the ball right along the ground with the clubhead, all the while keeping the effective loft of the clubface reduced by moving your hands out in front of it through impact. To facilitate this relationship in the impact area, it is important that you address the ball back in your stance, more toward your right foot, and have the sense—a very distinct sense—of your hands, and particularly your left hand, leading the swing very strongly through the impact area. When the clubhead is not allowed to catch up to your hands in the hitting area, its effective loft is reduced. Thus you're able to hit a low driving shot, or what is commonly termed a punch shot.

Each type of shot described can be exaggerated or kept to a minimum. If you want to keep a drive down, you would move the ball back slightly, not to an extreme as you would to stay under a tree.

In hitting a punch shot, the long hitting area that is encouraged by my style of swinging becomes very important, since it allows you to place your hands well in advance of the clubhead without worrying about squaring up the clubhead at impact. This is because, with my style, the clubhead is square and on line for a much longer period than is the case with most swing styles.

The key to good shotmaking—and to good golf for that matter—is developing a feel for where the clubface is during your swing, and understanding the exact position that you wish the clubface to be in at impact. If you sit down and carefully study the mechanics of hitting a hook, a fade, a high shot or a punch shot, you will begin to understand the exact relationships among swing line, clubface and target line; that must be established in order to hit a particular shot. All of the positions are basically logical. Once you have a proper understanding of these simple mechanical points, it becomes possible to adjust your alignment position and your swing pattern to provide for a proper relationship of directions at impact, allowing you to produce many more well-thought-out and well-executed golf shots.

13

A Golfer's Attitude

People everywhere, even people involved with golf, will say that a player choked—but who's to say when a player's choked? The player could simply have hit a bad shot and his nervous system quite possibly had nothing to do with it. Remember that you have to be an awfully good player even to get into a position where you can lose an important golf tournament. I don't like the word "choke." I do think, however, that you can get so nervous that you do not perform. You can be keyed up to a point where you cannot respond physically. Now if that means that you've choked, then I'm sure a lot of players do it. When I find myself feeling particularly nervous, I just talk to myself. I try to concentrate more on my work instead of the situation. It's the very same situation as hitting the shots that you don't enjoy playing. Put your concentration away from your nerves or problems and maybe the negative thoughts will roll away and maybe you'll forget them. A good part of the time you *will* forget them. If you can put your concentration into a very keyed-up moment—if you can put your concentration on the shots you have to play instead of the reward or the defeat that those shots might bring you —I think your chances are much better. It's a matter of controlling your emotions, not of getting rid of them. I don't believe you can get rid of them. I don't think that you can change your basic body chemistry and mental chemistry. I think it's there to stay with you and you just have to learn how to handle it. I believe nervousness and that sort of thing are a result of allowing your thinking to wander from the present, away from the task at hand. Once you begin to worry about consequences or past mistakes, you are inviting a bad case of nerves. No golfer can do any more than make the best of what he or she finds to be the immediate problem. Even if you're not

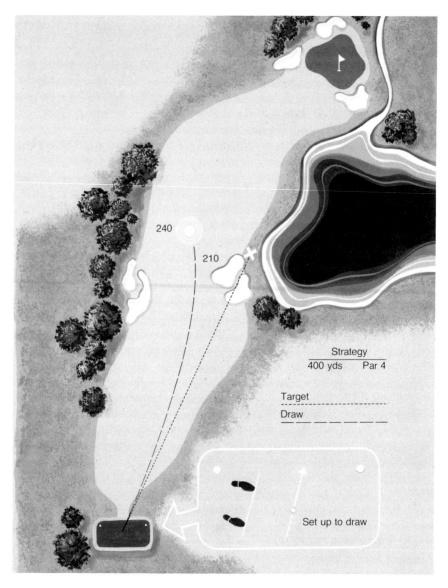

240

210

Strategy

400 yds   Par 4

Target

Draw

Set up to draw

A proper mental attitude is greatly aided by a feeling of assurance when standing over a golf shot. Often you will find that your overwhelming tendency on a particular day is either to draw or fade every shot, no matter what the circumstance. Even when you are faced with a hole that demands a shot of the opposite shape than the one that you feel comfortable with, you will probably be better off hitting your normal shot, be it a draw or a fade, even if it means starting the ball at the edge of a hazard.

happy about having to hit a certain shot, you must allow your mind to concentrate on the execution of that shot to the best of your ability. You may not be pleased with the circumstance, but you have to do the best thing possible as far as choosing and playing a shot is concerned.

Also along this line of thought is the problem of bad or upsetting conditions. Rather than thinking of the annoying aspect of a situation, you should think of the execution of the best shot possible. In that way you can put the unsettling factors out of your mind. We would all love to play under ideal conditions with good partners on nothing but beautiful golf courses, but among golf course owners, club members and superintendents, nobody strives for a poorly conditioned course, and you don't really gain anything by coming out with derogatory remarks. Golf is a game, it's a sport; some people play it for fun and some people play it competitively, but no one is forced to play it. So when you get to a place to play, whatever it is—it may be the worse-conditioned course you have ever seen in your life—simply accept what is there. If it affects you that badly, don't play.

The question of proper attitude extends to the moment when you strike the ball. It's not enough to accept and carefully consider what is before you if you can't bring your attention to the heart of the matter: hitting the shot. Everything that you might want to think about before playing a shot should be thought of and gotten out of the way before you step up to the ball. Your mind must be free and clear to look at the ball and help you to hit it. Make certain you take the time to erase all doubts from your mind before playing away.

You have to stand up to the ball with the club you feel the most comfortable with. Whether it be your second, third or first choice, you will probably not hit a good shot if you have any misgivings. You shouldn't be standing up to the ball with a club that you don't have faith in, trying to hit a shot that you don't have faith in. The only time you should try to hit with a club that you don't want to hit with or a shot that you don't want to hit is when you are absolutely forced to and there is no alternative. Otherwise, you should stand up with the club that feels best to you.

Somebody said once that he could hit a 1-iron as far as he thought he could hit a 1-iron. When I see the green, if it looks like a 1-iron to me at 210 yards, perhaps under most circumstances I can't hit it that far, but I *will* hit it that far because I think I can. There is so much comfort in doing what your sixth sense feels it should do. I think many times you can hit a better shot with the wrong club if you think it is right than you can with the right club if it is strictly against your nature to hit it. All of these things are involved in this method of making the game a little simpler and trying not to fight every natural instinct that you have.

You can't clutter your mind with too much thought because that's self-destructive. Assume that you are playing in competition—at this point I think you have to have practiced enough and you have to have your swing well-grooved enough that its variables are not an overriding factor in the day's play. There may have been one little thought that helped you to smooth it out, one little thought here and there that is really helpful at the time. Sometimes one little thought is a very good thing to have. It gives you something to concentrate on other than the upsetting aspects of the situation. To think about the actual positions and movements of your swing, though, is somewhat paralyzing. It takes away power and clubhead speed, and I think it forces you to come up with the little saving moves that you make during the middle of a swing. But there are times in competitive play when you are just having a bad day and you can't hit the ball, when physically there is something a little bit off-center, and you cannot hit it. Now on a day like that, there are ways to get the ball around the course, to shoot a round that does not put you out of the tournament. But a day like that requires discipline. I suppose it also requires the sense to accept the fact that you don't have all the physical ability that you had yesterday. Maybe it will come back tomorrow, but today it is gone. And with the knowledge that maybe you're not as strong, maybe you're not moving as well today, maybe you're not as loose today as you were yesterday—with that knowledge and a little bit of concentration—I think you can work the ball around well enough to where you're not out of it after the first day. It's very depressing: you spend the rest of the tournament fighting it and trying to get back in it, and it's such an uphill battle that most of the time it's impossible. Once you're in trouble —when you hit a shot into trouble—what should you think? Accept the fact that you're in trouble, but remember that in most cases you will still have a shot. It's very common for somebody to walk up and ask, "Oh, why am I here?" and he or she will go backwards mentally, back on the tee. I think the most important thing in that situation is to figure out what you can do from here, in the present, and not to worry about what you already did. It's constructive when you hit a bad shot to make a little mental note of the bad thoughts you had or the bad movements you made that got you in trouble—just a little note so that it doesn't happen again—a small way of avoiding repetition of the experience. No matter what the situation, you can't let the emotions of the bad shot ruin the next shot. By the time you arrive at the next shot, the last shot has to be erased. You have a whole new problem in front of you, and you have to work that problem out. The fact that you are there cannot be changed. I think it's hard to feel nothing at all; I think it's a bit inhuman. So you are going to feel something. The important thing is to feel it, make a note of it, then get rid of it—because you have to go on. At this point your next move is more important than the shot you already played. Often you see people that hit a slice off the tee and then they say, "I knew I was going to do that." They do that in their effort not to do it. But you see a more experienced player come along, and a hole can be set up such that it doesn't quite appeal to that player, and he or she may feel as though it's not going to be a very good shot. But an experienced player will not dwell on the difficulty, and will think only of the shot to be made and the task at hand. That sort of thinking makes the game much more manageable and less frustrating. It lessens your chance of defeating yourself internally.

Try to put your concentration on the place you would like to go—the intended target—instead of on the trouble you are trying to avoid.

V

For Women Only

14

For Women Only

One of the most obvious problems that women have is that so few of them can reach holes in regulation figures. This demands a great deal of their short game. They are always trying to press in their long games, trying to get more than they have. I think women need to hit the ball a little further off the tee. They need to be expert wedge players because they need it so many times to make a par on the longer holes. The biggest problem I see for women when driving the ball is that, as graceful and as rhythmic as they are supposed to be, their balance is poor. I see too many women who make a great lunging effort to hit the ball hard. With such a great lunging effort you need superb balance.

I think that a good illustration of the importance of balance is seen in the play of Chako Higuchi on the LPGA tour. Chako has a sizable lateral sway in her swing, and most people, when watching her, are amazed at how well she hits the ball. The absolute key to her success is balance, and it is because she is so solidly planted on her feet at impact that she is able to play so well with an unorthodox swing style. In contrast, most women amateurs that I watch are so off balance during the swing and at impact that there is little if any chance of their hitting the ball with power.

With all these lunging moves, I think a woman tends to strike down on her driver. And a woman, most of all, needs to sweep the ball off the tee to transmit all the clubhead speed she can. By working on positioning the ball at address and by making sure you're very solid on your feet, you are free to have a little movement without losing your balance. Just those two things should enable a woman to take a little bit more of a man-size cut at the ball and at the same time create some clubhead speed. And with a driver, when you have the ball sitting on a little wooden peg, it just isn't necessary. Anyway, if you could give a lot of women fifteen to twenty yards off the tee—which isn't really a lot, when you consider that they're not driving the ball a long way to start with—it would make a great difference in their games.

A woman's anatomy is naturally somewhat different from a man's. Except in extraordinary cases you can generally get around the problem of anatomy by the way you set up. I think a woman can stand too close to the ball so that she restricts any turning movement. The bend at the hip that we talk about is an important thing because it sets you up in a position where you have some freedom of movement. Turning is a big factor. If you turn away from the ball you're not going to get in your own way too much. If you make disjointed moves away from the ball, you are going to get all tangled up with yourself. And the fact of the matter is, if you can get away from the ball into a position where you're coiled to strike at the ball, then your problems are over.

One of the things contributing to women's anatomy problems that you see either terribly exaggerated or not at all is what I call "extending the left arm." You either see a woman with a terribly stiff left arm, that she couldn't move if she had to, or one with no extension at all. A good extension of the left arm at address will help with a woman's anatomy problems. The whole picture of a good setup would help that particular problem more than anything I know. The poor setup requires a lot of body manipulation.

One of the factors limiting the power of women is that so few of them get any kind of a good weight shift along with their turn. I think that if they did, they would find the turn pretty easy. Everybody is trying to move into the ball, but you can't move into the ball until you've set yourself up to do it. In fact, all this emphasis on moving into the ball can really hurt you. If you don't turn back properly, it can move you right past the ball and over it if you haven't done the proper things to begin with. Women really need to be behind the ball at the top of the backswing. They need to learn how to use their legs; but none of them will learn how to use their legs until they learn how to coil themselves behind the ball correctly. If you would just do these simple things, getting behind the ball at impact in many cases would take care of itself. The idea is to get that weight moving at impact, and the only way to get it moving at impact is to begin behind the ball at the top of the backswing. Then it will be moving with the release of the club. Actually, when you finally get down to it, your weight is moving at impact because the lower part of your body is in such high gear. The weight is actually moving a little bit ahead of the ball—it's a little bit past impact as you're releasing the club—but it has set up the release. And with the lower half of your body driving, you've set up the upper half behind the ball to be the follower.

You've got to pay attention to the preliminaries to achieve all these things. In fact, in this particular sense I would say the preliminaries of the backswing and the takeaway are the most important. Because in many cases if you can get that far, the rest will help itself along.

One thing on wedge play that strikes me as being important for women is that your weight should basically be toward your left side when you're pitching. I've already talked about how you want a minimum of movement, and that helps. But women tend to hit the little low-bladed shot, or the little fat shot, far too often. Your weight should never be even on both feet for short shots. You should even find yourself listing to the left side, I would say, no more than forty to sixty per cent. The object is to have a place that is solid to set up on. This will minimize your movement. I think that with the weight over on the left side, it's a little easier to learn how to flush the ball and hit the ball first with a short shot.

Strategy is a big problem with women, too. Most courses aren't designed for the woman club player, and a lot of trouble, plus certain things that aren't even supposed to come into play, come into play for them. Or perhaps some of the things that are *supposed* to come into play on a golf course don't for them. But it's a whole different course from the front tees and especially when you're hitting the ball no great distance. A woman—or anyone for that matter—has to learn to play within herself. But I see too many women who have learned to play so well within themselves that there's no longer an aggressive bone in their bodies. If they are happy to play like that, that's fine. But that kind of woman player could learn to shave a few strokes off by being a little more aggressive, taking a more forceful cut at the ball. I think her approach could be improved upon. The ideal thing for every player is to be an intelligent, aggressive player, to know when it is to advantage to be aggressive. To know, when there is very little risk involved, that you must hit an aggressive shot. And to know how to hit a positive shot when there is a risk to consider. For some women, when they have a little shot over water after hitting all the way down the fairway, when all of a sudden the water is there, they can no longer do it. That's like leaving a pie in the oven after taking an hour to do a bang-up job of preparing it! This is one time you have to concentrate on what you have to do to hit the shot well, not on what you've got to do to get the ball over the water. I'm a strong believer in hitting the ball solidly. I think it cures so many ailments. If women would just concentrate on making solid contact with the ball, a good many common faults would be corrected. If you're one of the people who mis-hits

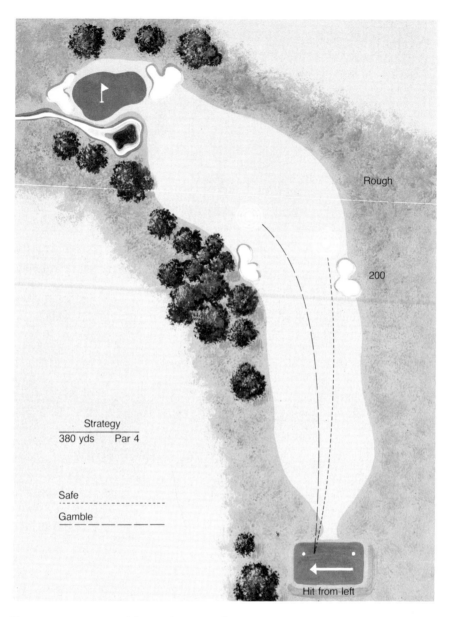

Rough

200

Strategy
380 yds   Par 4

Safe

Gamble

Hit from left

Most women are too quick to select the safest possible shot, even when they have a perfect opportunity to be aggressive. If you are faced with a hole that curves in the direction of your natural shot pattern, don't neglect the advantage that you've been given. Rather than aiming away from the trouble and contenting yourself with an average position from the tee, try to allow your natural shot to take the ball around the corner of the dogleg in position for an aggressive second shot.

the ball and comes off the ball a lot, concentrate on the back of the ball and you'll be surprised at what a different feeling it is—and how easily the trajectory of the shot changes. The ball is immediately airborne with no effort from you. Any time you strike the ball flush on a club with any amount of loft, the ball will go up. But too often there is too much manipulating and the loft of the club is changed, or you hit very high on the ball, or you hit the ground first. I find that even for myself, when I need to hit the ball a little better than I have been, concentrating on the back of the ball helps.

Also, keying on the back of the ball is not a bad practice exercise. It encourages the player to be behind the ball. It's always difficult to hit the back of the ball when you're over the top of it or when you're coming at it from the outside. Just as an exercise, to encourage your body to stay behind it, it's a good thing to concentrate on.

The one thing I didn't go into when I was discussing the swing, but that I believe in a lot, is something I think of when I'm teaching and even when I am helping myself: that your body is kind of separated into two pieces. You have the upper part of your body and the lower part of your body. I always speak of the left side of the body being the strong side or the leader and the right side being the weak side or the follower. In the same vein, I think the lower part of your body is the strong part and the upper part has to be the weaker part. The upper part of your body, like the right side, has to be the follower. I think most of the major moves in your swing are initiated by the lower part of your body. Some players who look good have that kind of fluidity, because at impact the lower part of the body is driving well ahead of the ball. And the other part of the body is well behind the ball. But trying to teach someone who's never done it before is very difficult. To achieve that position is very difficult. And women, because of their anatomy, should be able to understand and achieve this better than men. But they don't for some reason—I'm not sure why. Because there is such a separation between the upper and lower body in the female anatomy these are things that women should be able to feel and do. When I speak of the lower part of the body initiating the swing, I also think that the lowest part of the lower part of the body initiates the swing. I think that your feet and your legs driving at impact make it look as if your hips are driving at impact. I don't ever try to make a conscious hip effort. Most of the conscious effort is in moving the weight. Because I make the effort to get most of it to the right side during the backswing, I have to move back to the left during the downswing. So if I'm going to know where my weight is, I have to feel it with my feet and begin the transfer of the weight with my feet and legs. I don't consciously push off my right side, but then it's not something I haven't worked on at times. I try not to do anything very consciously with my right side. However, I do try to leave my right side free to work when its time comes. But I'm definitely a right-handed person, so I don't have to tell my right side to go.

I think the idea that women players are better short-game players than men is a fallacy. If you compare the men's tour and the women's tour you will see that the men have better short games than the women. I don't mean to say that the women aren't great hitters of the ball. But I often see the men play some beautiful wedge shots. I think the women are much better long putters than the men. Their touch may be a little bit better. But as far as the actual execution of many shots, the men are probably superior.

For years women have been given credit for being fantastic short-game players; I think the truth of the matter is that a lot of the women on the tour score well because they hit the ball well. Not that they don't have good short games, but the short game is not necessarily the saving factor for every player out there. In fact, watching a player like Mickey Wright, you can't honestly say that her short game was ever superior. I don't think my short game is exceptional. I would say that there are some women who are absolute artists from a hundred yards in. But I'm talking about women and men professionals in general. I think the men are simply better at this particular phase of the game. It seems to me wrong that they should be, logically speaking, but I think they are. I may be wrong about this, but I think the men may have a few more opportunities to play those hundred-yard shots and shorter shots. I think many times we're a little further away than that, whereas the men are hitting wedges and 9-irons to a few par-4 holes simply because of their unbelievable length. We don't run into that very often. The women are most often going to get the hundred-yard shot only on the par-5s.

It's not even a point of discussion that a woman should tend towards a stronger grip when all women in unison tell you that they can't create enough clubhead speed, and when no more than half of one per cent of the women in the world who play golf can hit the ball far enough. With golf courses built as they are, everything has to be done to get the ball out there further and with a certain amount of control.

I think women should adopt the most natural putting stance possible. But in putting there are, of course, certain exceptions to every rule. Any address position that an individual prefers should naturally be close to the type of position that is very easy to repeat. If it's something way out of the ordinary, I'm not saying you can't do it—because you can—but you have to make sure that the position is comfortable enough for you that it is an easy position to repeat over and over again. One of the biggest tricks to putting is to be able to repeat all facets of the setup and the stroke. If your address position can't be repeated, it is a fairly good bet that it will be difficult to repeat your stroke.

There isn't a great deal to tell women specifically about putting. There are a lot of women who have an awfully good touch, who are good putters. This might sound like a very minor point, but I do see many women who lay the putterhead down behind the ball just in the general direction of the hole. How big is a hole? A little over four inches. It's a fairly small diameter and there's not much margin for error, so I think that the lining up of that blade should be much more deliberate. In putting, the general direction simply won't get it. It's not really something that I or anyone else should have to tell a golfer, but the simplest things are often overlooked in this game. You have to be told and then you have to understand these things before you become fully aware of them.

Women in general don't seem to pay quite as much attention to reading greens as they could. I don't think that they can't read greens. So many mistakes that you make can be eliminated by your preliminary work. By this I mean that during the time before setting yourself up to the ball, whether it be to a putt, a chip or whatever, you can eliminate a lot of potential mistakes by careful thinking.

Many good players say that the way they get into a number of their swing problems, or the reason that they fall into a slump, is that somehow their address position or their setup pattern has changed without their realizing it. Now these are people who very possibly play golf for a living, so you know they're constantly aware of it. But the minute that your setup changes—whether you are putting, hitting a drive or anything else—all of a sudden your alignment changes. This is just the kind of thing that throws a swing off, though there really isn't any reason for a professional's swing to change. That swing has been functioning the same way for perhaps twenty years, so there has to be a very basic explanation for why it has suddenly altered. The player who has always been a good hitter has a week where all of a sudden he or she can't hit the ball at all. A lot of good players agree that their setup and their alignment have an awful lot to do with how well they swing at the ball and for how long a period of time they can stay at their peak.

I don't know if this is peculiar to me, but when I'm driving I tend more and more to set up a little bit more to the right because I really feel like I'm going to crunch it, swing way out away from myself. I think that all women should attempt to hook the ball with the driver, simply because of the distance that is gained. With this in mind, I would prefer to see a woman set up in a slightly closed position for the longer shots. It has worked well for men for long periods of time, but when it goes too far—when I'm not moving quite as fast as I was before and I'm not at a peak of performance as far as swinging the club—the first thing I have to do is go back and set myself up more squarely to the target, realign myself and then work up to that peak again. You can get carried away with things that feel good, particularly when you're hitting the ball well. For instance, you start aiming just a hair down the right side of the fairway because it feels so good just to hit it as hard as you can and to have complete faith that it will come back perfectly to the center. Then you go along for a while and you're really driving the ball well and all of a sudden you think, "Well, if I can drive it so well from that setup, perhaps I can set up a little more to the right and *really* crack it." Pretty soon you've got yourself out of position and you're not cracking it at all anymore. That's what I mean by getting carried away. You can take a good thing too far. You have to know your capabilities, particularly when you are playing competitive golf. As I said one other time, you have to be able to *play aggressively within yourself.*

I still do take a closed stance to the ball at times, and I'm not against it for any reason. At times it's a more comfortable position for me. The biggest reason I don't have to exaggerate it too much is that I have been so well trained to extend the clubhead out away from me that, if I'm not a little bit careful, I tend to hit the ball out to the right of the target. What I tend to do, in effect, for people who know golf terms, is to block the shot a little. I tend not to let my hands release. I make a subconscious effort to keep my hands from releasing. I make no conscious attempt to restrain the release, but sometimes I encourage that kind of mistake if I close up too much. It's funny, because when I was young, a few great players saw me hit a ball, or saw a picture of me, they all said the day would come when I'd really have trouble with a hook. And the fact of the matter is I have never had any serious trouble hooking. A couple of times I have had a little bit of trouble leaving the ball to the right—I mean actually hitting it to the right. It's not a cut shot, where I'm curving it to the right; it actually flies straight to the right of the target and I'm not able to do much about it. It turned out that all the experts were one hundred per cent wrong about what would happen with a strong left-hand grip.

You know, I think it's really an interesting problem that there are women who are built similarly to some men, whether the man be small or the woman large, and—it's really a mystery to me why it is—that women don't have the physical strength that men have. But they simply do not. That's a fact. I've read one article that attributes some of the difference to the fact that boys mature late, that their bones have a longer time to develop, and that they are actually of a stronger bone structure. I don't know whether all that is medically correct, but it made a little bit of sense to me.

To give a specific example, at one time Bob Toski was helping me a great deal; I had gained a little weight and I think we were something like eight pounds apart. Even though I was driving the ball a long way for me at the time, I could never hit the ball as far as Bob. I would guess that the closest I ever got was within twenty or twenty-five yards, when he was hitting the ball well. It's just an amazing thing. One day in an awfully big wind that really blew, down in the Florida Keys at Ocean Reef, we were playing from the same tees, and under the circumstances I thought that the 74 I shot was a pretty good round. Bob shot 64, beat me by ten shots. It was interesting.

Bob never could understand why anyone who had the balance of movement in the golf swing that I had wasn't a very good dancer. But he always used to tell people that it was like dancing, and to be light on their feet but very well balanced. Of course he was a great example of all those things.

Clubhead speed is the biggest inadequacy of women club golfers. They don't understand, with as much effort they put into the swing, why the club doesn't whip through faster, why they can't swish the air like somebody else can. It's the root of a lot of their problems. I think they realize that without clubhead speed you can't hit the ball very far. The best way that I know of alleviating that is to teach a woman how to make better use of her entire body, of everything she has. By teaching her, number one, to make a bigger arc. Very few women do make the kind of arc that they're capable of. I think the feeling of a somewhat flatter plane helps to develop clubhead speed. And I think learning how to use your hands, how to set them up so that they can release—a combination of all these things would really help the average woman golfer.

I think women grip the club too tightly and instead of creating speed with firmness they create tension. Often the problem is in their equipment. This may require a little money, but one of the most important things I do to my clubs is change the grips once a year. I think a slick grip is really detrimental to hitting the ball well. There is too much thought, whether conscious or subconscious, to not lose the grip somewhere along the way. And I think it's really worth the little bit that it costs to have new, soft grips put on, particularly to someone who takes the game very seriously. Overnight it can change the way you feel standing over the ball. Slick grips just make for tension. You feel tension and you feel fear that you're going to lose the grip. You just can't react the same. A firm feeling with the grip is so important. I lick my glove a lot, which makes people look twice—but it's not very ladylike for a woman to spit on her glove! So I give it a little touch with my tongue.

Aside from grips, there are other important equipment factors that a woman should be aware of. Longer clubs, in particular, would be a great help to most women. Be careful, though, when you try longer clubs, that they are not too heavy to handle. Try experimenting with a very light men's set, or at least with a longer driver. Mine is an inch longer even than standard men's length.

Women have to be particularly good planners. And after you've become a good planner, the key is to believe in your plan. If your plan is to lay up short of the water, take the club out that will put you short of the water and don't be afraid to hit it. Once you have made the decision ("I'm going to lay up to the water with this 6-iron") then just be sure you do. Hit the shot with assurance.

Not too long ago in El Paso I saw a lady who was ten yards off a fairway bunker. It was fairly close to the green, but it wasn't set at the green. She could still land short of the green and put the ball on the green. And she asked me to come over and teach her how to get that ball over the bunker. She was hitting a full 9-iron, but she had such a negative state of mind. And I told her that once she'd decided what club she was going to hit, she should forget the sand trap was even there. This was at an exhibition at Coronado Country Club in El Paso. She was a cute little lady with an Irish accent, an older lady, and it was really enlightening. And the minute she concentrated on hitting the ball, she hit the ball very well. As it happened, she put the ball in another trap up by the green, but the other trap wasn't the problem at the time. She had chosen the wrong club, but she still hit the ball well. It's just a matter of where your concentration is. If your concentration is on the trap, you're going to swing scared and will probably hit a poor shot. If your concentration is on striking the ball, or hitting the ball flush, how are you going to put it in the trap? You're not.

I would advise any woman player who spends any time at all practicing to practice the key shots that will help her to score. Driving, needless to say, is particularly critical. The further that she can get it off the tee, the better off she'll be. I think that any woman who's striving for more clubhead speed should get more of a feeling that the club is not an immovable part of her. Most women look a little bit stiff to me, and a little bit like they are trying to steer the clubhead back to the ball. That's really restrictive. If you get yourself set up at the ball fairly well and you have any feel at all, and you can use the extension of your left arm as a measure, then there is no reason why you shouldn't hit the ball squarely. In fact, there is more chance that you won't make contact with it when trying very hard to, than if you simply employ the methods of extending and swinging the club through to the target. In a way, you want the ball to get in the way of the clubhead instead of the clubhead getting to the ball. The thought that the ball is going to get in the way of the clubhead makes certain that the clubhead is moving. It's not steered and you're not trying to direct it.

Too many women think that the shot is over when contact is made; actually it's only half over. So you're going to hit half a shot if impact is where you stop your effort. To create sufficient clubhead speed, the club has to be traveling very freely at impact. If you do that, it can't possibly stop until you're two-thirds of the way into the followthrough. And your follow-through is actually a relaxing action after the centrifugal force of the club swinging around you and through the ball has been spent. That's why I don't think followthroughs should be posed positions. I think it's the relaxed position you fall into naturally after you've generated the speed.

Back to things I was saying about women practicing. Again, if you do practice at all, you should practice the particular things that would help you to score, those things being (besides driving and putting) possibly 5-wood shots, definitely wedge shots, and any of the little shots around the green. Women can play pretty well and still not reach most of the greens. If they would learn to get the ball up and down a certain percentage of the time, their opportunities for lower scoring would be greatly improved. I find that women are better chippers than pitchers. If they don't have to be too concerned with getting the ball up in the air they are pretty confident. I think ball position is the determining factor with many of them. Too much has been taught and written about getting your hands ahead of the ball. For goodness' sake, with a short club, if you address the ball properly and you just let your hands fall, they will be ahead of the ball.

It's not simply a matter of having your hands forward. Half the women who play golf and don't have enough knowledge of it have their hands forward, and lose about ten or fifteen degrees of the loft built into the club every time they shove their hands up front. They are not getting the benefit of the design of the club. I don't think putting your hands ahead of the ball is a thing that takes very conscious effort. It's a thing that naturally happens if the ball is addressed properly and the address position is determined by the length of the club. As the clubs get shorter, the hands fall a little bit more forward. That's simply the way the club is built. Any time you push your hands way forward you're sitting the club on its leading edge. The club should sit flush on its sole.

Women should be very conscious of proper ball position. Keep the ball off your left heel and learn to choke down on the club a little when you are inside of what would normally be a full shot. This will give you more control. Learn to get your weight a little more toward the left side for short shots; it will help you to stay more still. A lot of missed wedge shots are bladed, a mistake caused by movement. And the last thing you can work on, which you should be able to work on at all times, is finding a comfortable tempo. Find one that feels good to you and one you can remember in your mind's eye and muscle memory.

A lot of women focus so much attention on the takeaway that they forget all about the overall tempo of the swing. Everybody says you've got to take it away slow. If you take it away too slowly, the instinctive reaction will be to speed up. Excessive deliberation makes you unable to generate the energy to accelerate, for the clubhead to gradually move faster. What it makes for is a sudden pickup when it has to get faster, and that creates some kind of a jerk or a jump. I think some people's takeaways will naturally be faster than others. But what they all should be is relaxed. If there is such a thing as controlled relaxation, that's what it should be. Nothing should be so tense so as to force yourself to think to make yourself move. But then again, you should always have complete control of what the clubhead does and of what your hands do. Not that you're going to force them to make a lot of moves, but you'll have control of them. You are going to control the club, and you are going to let the clubhead do the work.

Because most women do not have the natural physical power that allows men to get away with a less than perfect golf swing, it is very important that women be particularly well acquainted with the physical mechanics of the swing. I know of no better way to give the muscles an opportunity to learn the movements of the golf swing than allowing them to experience the feel of a well-executed swing.

Most golfers are so tense and frantic when they are trying to cure a fault on the practice tee that they force their bodies to adopt certain very unnatural positions instead of allowing the muscles to move freely with the swinging of the club. The body is much more comfortable when it is being guided by feel rather than by thought. That is what Hogan was speaking of when he used the term "muscle memory."

Instead of relying entirely on actual practice to learn the feel of a good swing, I think that most golfers, particularly women, would feel less pressure learning the swing using a program of simple exercises. Not only will these exercises strengthen and train the important golfing muscles but they will be more apt to change habits, because the player does not have the flight of the ball to worry about and will be more likely to let the muscles go and have their own way.

If we can break the swing down into its important parts, it is possible to train the body piece by piece until a proper swing becomes almost second nature to the muscles. For most women, the gain in strength that will naturally come with these exercises might just be the biggest thing that they can do to help their game.

Exercises

Three basic exercises to strengthen a woman's game. By swinging from one foot to the other, you rapidly learn the feeling of moving your weight smoothly and fully through the ball.

Holding a club to which a brick has been tied, roll the brick up and down using only your hands and wrists. This will develop a great deal of strength in your wrists and forearms.

By simply raising a club directly in front of you with your left hand and wrist, you can develop your left hand naturally as the controlling hand during the swing.

The exercise to learn balance and weight shift is a good one. I take the club back and I lift my left foot; then when I get the club through, I'm able to lift my right foot, the idea being to show the weight shift and to feel it. It's pretty difficult to do at first, but after a while you can do it and feel fairly well balanced. In that respect it gives you both the feeling of your weight moving and the feeling of good balance. I've finally gotten to where I can hit the ball pretty well doing this. And I can do it with practically no movement from side to side. You don't slide off the ball to move your weight. That is not to say that your head has to be totally stationary, but you should strive for a very minimum of movement.

To do this first exercise, I start lifting the left foot when I'm almost to the top of the swing, while I'm in motion. It's a difficult thing to do when you're taking a club up to the top and you're just trying to lift one leg. But that's the beauty of it—you have to be in motion to do it well. When you get to the top, you lift the left and at the finish the right.

When I was a little girl I learned this next exercise. You just take a golf club in one hand and hold it straight out in front of you, with your arm straight out away from you. Then move the club straight up so that it's pointing straight at the sky, but only move the club with your wrists, and only move your wrists in the same way that you want your wrists to cock in the golf swing. Needless to say, you don't put your left hand on the club with a strong left-hand grip because you don't want the hands to move around the body taking the club up. But you put your hand on the club in very much the same position that you'd shake hands with someone. Your thumb is facing up. And it's an exercise to strengthen your wrist and forearm a little bit. You can do it with both hands for that matter, but most women work on developing their left hand a little more, because their right hand is usually fairly well developed from all the normal use it gets.

I would strongly recommend any little exercise to strengthen your legs. I wouldn't go in for weight lifting or anything like that, because then you're developing muscles that you don't use so much in your chest and shoulders. What I'm trying to say is that the muscles you want to develop are the little, seldom-used muscles, not the big muscles.

At one time we had a lead pipe, and there was a rope around the middle and at the end of the rope was tied a brick, and I would roll the brick up and let the brick down in an effort to strengthen my forearms. Did it do any good? Well, I'm a lot stronger than I look.

A simple exercise you can do if you're really trying to strengthen your forearms, your hands and fingers is to lay a sheet of newspaper out and start with one hand resting on a corner of the paper. Use your fingers to pull it in. Get the whole thing into a ball in your hand. Just by reaching with your fingers and pulling it in you will develop strength in your hands. I think this is a particularly good exercise if you want results in a month or so. It would have to help you.

The best thing you can do for a tempo exercise is to swing a weighted club, because you cannot jerk a really heavy club. The only bad thing about this is when you get back to your normal club it seems so light to you that it's almost easier to swing it too quickly. Sometimes a heavy club is a good little warmup club, if swung three or four times before you hit off the tee. But to work with it constantly makes your own normal club feel too light and I think it tends to make you jerky.

Swinging two clubs prior to going out to play is also a useful device to loosen you up. I don't know that it's good for anything else, because when you're stiff and tight your clubs feel kind of heavy and after that kind of action they don't feel so heavy to you. I very rarely play without warming up on the practice tee, one reason being that I like to start off playing well. Secondly, I don't want to take a chance of hurting myself; even as much as I play, that's possible. So I warm up a little bit before I play. A lot of golfers don't have the time for that. If you don't have the time for that, you shouldn't expect too much of yourself on the first hole. But a warmup session doesn't have to be a big thing. If you can go out and hit ten balls, it makes a big difference. You don't have to take an hour, you can take ten minutes. Anything that puts your hands on the club. One part of you that's stiff when you first start out is your hands. They're not used to holding a golf club. They haven't been in the grip position all night and all day and perhaps longer. Anything to put your hands on the club and give you the feeling of making contact with the ball. Again, a woman playing golf must take advantage of planning and think well if she is to play to her potential. Don't put yourself at a disadvantage before you even swing a club.

What I hope to have done in writing this book is to make it simpler for you to understand the mechanical and mental aspects of the game, and thereby make it possible for you to improve as a golfer. I am convinced that there are some very sound reasons why an unathletic person such as myself can play golf at the highest levels of competition and succeed. I have tried, in writing this book, to articulate those elements of my method that I feel are responsible for my competitive achievements. I realize, of course, that the large majority of the golfing population plays the game for fun, but I'm certain that by playing a better game most golfers will be able to derive a little more enjoyment from the sport.

Unfortunately, even the simpler parts of this game require a little thought and practice. I'm still rereading the putting section and trying to practice what I preach. Regardless of how quickly or slowly you progress, don't consider yourself hopeless or beyond improving. I have worked hard at this game for a quarter of a century, and I still have a great deal of work ahead of me. If all else fails and I encounter a woman who is just heart-broken over her golf game, I remind her that she probably does a number of things much better than I do, whether in her profession or in her kitchen.